Standard Grade | General

Mathematics

Abz

Leckie × Leckie

First exam published in 2003.
Published by Leckie & Leckie Ltd, 3rd Floor, 4 Queen Street, Edinburgh EH2 1JE
tel: 0131 220 6831 fax: 0131 225 9987 enquiries@leckieandleckie.co.uk www.leckieandleckie.co.uk

ISBN 978-1-84372-518-3

A CIP Catalogue record for this book is available from the British Library.

Printed in Scotland by Scotprint.

Leckie & Leckie is a division of Huveaux plc.

Leckie & Leckie is grateful to the copyright holders, as credited at the back of the book, for permission to use their material. Every effort has been made to trace the copyright holders and to obtain their permission for the use of copyright material. Leckie & Leckie will gladly receive information enabling them to rectify any error or omission in subsequent editions.

2003 | General

[BLANK PAGE]

FOR OFFICIAL USE

G

	KU	RE
Total marks		

2500/403

NATIONAL QUALIFICATIONS 2003

THURSDAY, 8 MAY
10.40 AM – 11.15 AM

MATHEMATICS STANDARD GRADE
General Level
Paper 1
Non-calculator

Fill in these boxes and read what is printed below.

Full name of centre

Town

Forename(s)

Surname

Date of birth

Day Month Year

Scottish candidate number

Number of seat

1 **You may <u>not</u> use a calculator.**

2 Answer as many questions as you can.

3 Write your working and answers in the spaces provided. Additional space is provided at the end of this question-answer book for use if required. If you use this space, write clearly the number of the question involved.

4 Full credit will be given only where the solution contains appropriate working.

5 Before leaving the examination room you must give this book to the invigilator. If you do not you may lose all the marks for this paper.

SCOTTISH QUALIFICATIONS AUTHORITY

FORMULAE LIST

Circumference of a circle:	$C = \pi d$
Area of a circle:	$A = \pi r^2$
Curved surface area of a cylinder:	$A = 2\pi rh$
Volume of a cylinder:	$V = \pi r^2 h$
Volume of a triangular prism:	$V = Ah$

Theorem of Pythagoras:

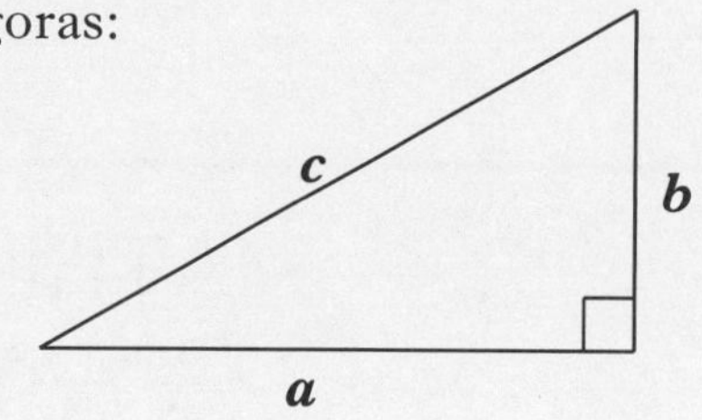

$$a^2 + b^2 = c^2$$

Trigonometric ratios in a right angled triangle:

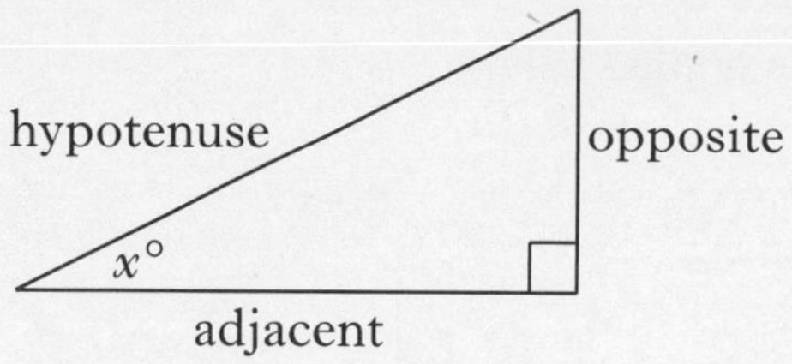

$$\tan x^\circ = \frac{\textbf{opposite}}{\textbf{adjacent}}$$

$$\sin x^\circ = \frac{\textbf{opposite}}{\textbf{hypotenuse}}$$

$$\cos x^\circ = \frac{\textbf{adjacent}}{\textbf{hypotenuse}}$$

Gradient:

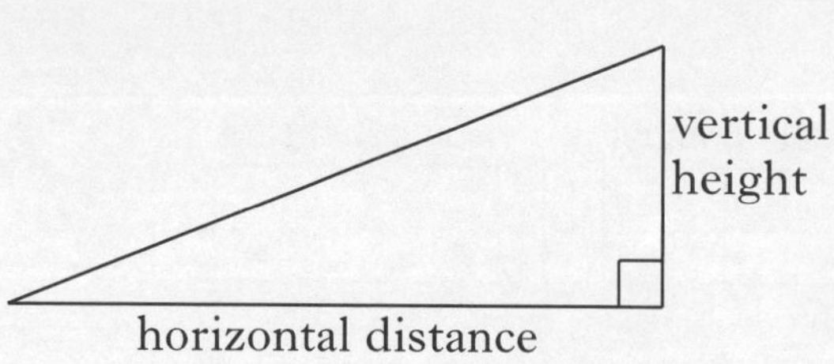

$$\textbf{Gradient} = \frac{\textbf{vertical height}}{\textbf{horizontal distance}}$$

DO NOT WRITE IN THIS MARGIN

Marks	KU	RE

1. Carry out the following calculations.

(*a*) 3·58 – 2·734

3.580
– 2.734
0·846

0.846

1

(*b*) 6·37 × 60

6.37 × 60

6.37 × 10 = 63.7

63.7 × 6 = 382·2

382.2

1

(*c*) 13·8 ÷ 4

4 ⟌ 13.8 = 03.4

3.45

1

(*d*) $\frac{3}{4} + \frac{1}{16}$

$\frac{6}{32} + \frac{8}{32}$

$\frac{14}{32} = \frac{7}{16}$

2

[Turn over

DO NOT WRITE IN THIS MARGIN

Marks | KU | RE

2. Bruce sets out from base during an orienteering competition.

The arrow in the sketch below shows the direction in which he is travelling.

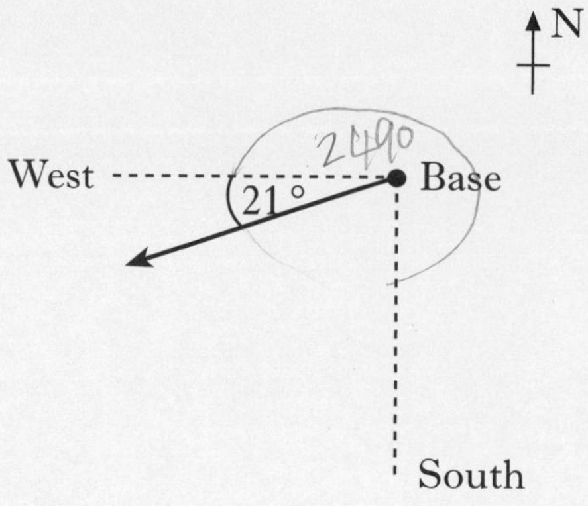

What is the three-figure bearing of this direction?

90 − 21 = 111   360 − 111 = 249

249°

2

3. Nine wooden balls numbered one to nine are placed in a bag.

A ball is removed from the bag.

What is the probability that this ball has a number more than 7?

$\frac{2}{9}$ 2 in 9 chances

2

DO NOT WRITE IN THIS MARGIN

Marks | KU | RE

4. The letter A is shown in the diagram.

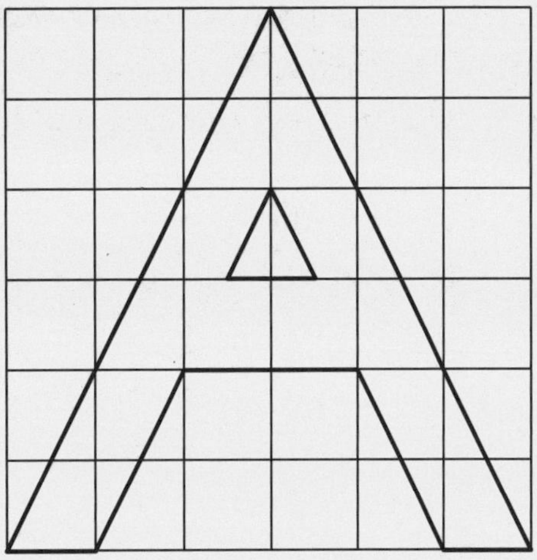

On the grid below, draw an enlargement of this letter A using a scale factor of 2.

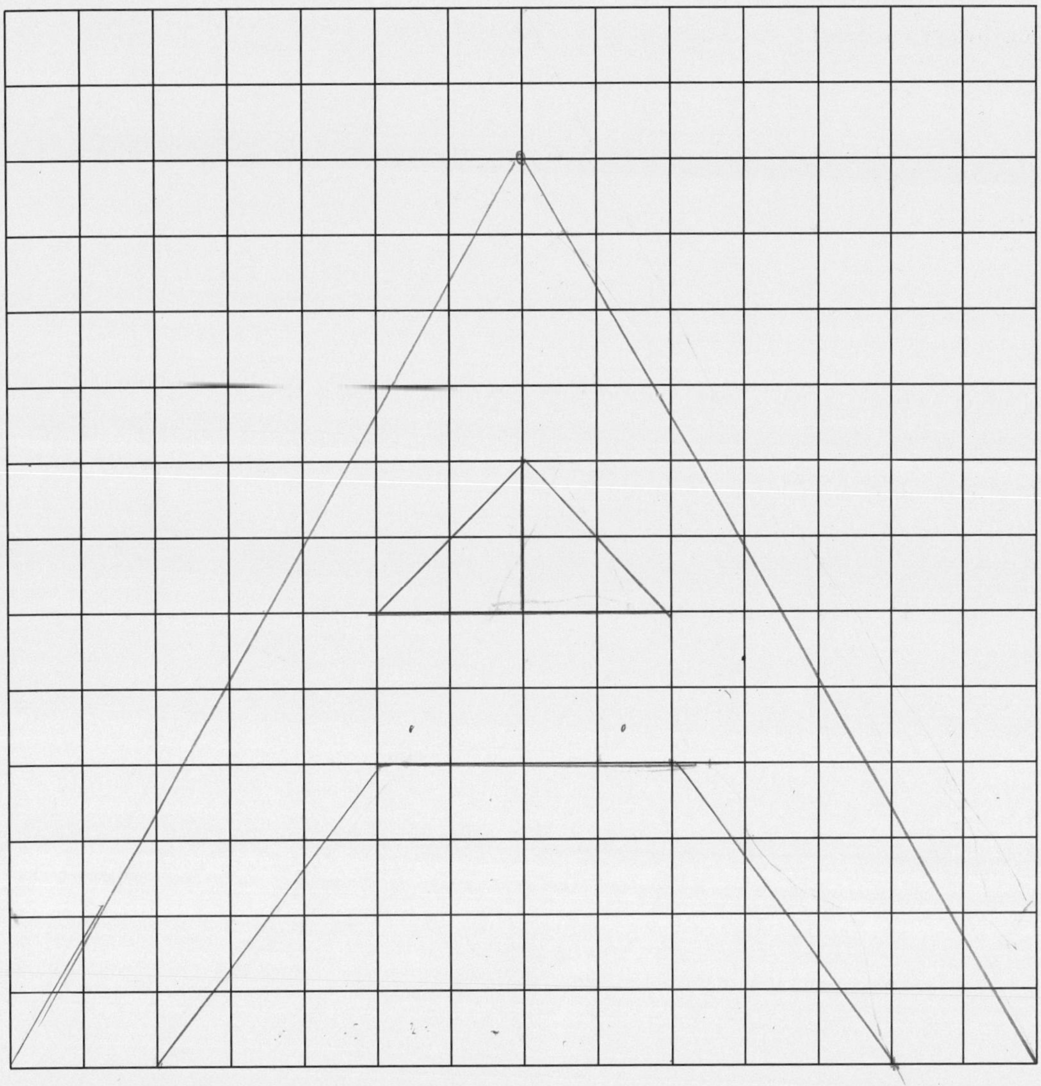

3

[Turn over

DO NOT WRITE IN THIS MARGIN

Marks | KU | RE

5. The number of hours of sunshine was recorded daily in a city during a three-week period in June.

The results are shown in the stem and leaf diagram below.

0	8
1	
2	1 3
3	2 5 7
4	1 5 7 8
5	2 3 6
6	0 2 2
7	1 1 3 7 9

n = 21

3 | 2 represents 3·2 hours

Using the above diagram:

(*a*) calculate the range; **2**

(*b*) find the median number of hours. **1**

DO NOT WRITE IN THIS MARGIN

Marks | KU | RE

6. Four friends have dinner in a restaurant.

A service charge of 15% is added to their bill.

Their bill is shown below.

Armando's Pizza Restaurant

4 medium Pizzas	£28·00
4 large Colas	£ 5·00
	£33·00
Total including 15% service charge	£38·95

One of the friends thinks the service charge has been calculated wrongly.

Is the service charge correct?

Give a reason for your answer.

15% of £33

10% of £33 = 33 ÷ 10 = 3.30

5% of £33 = (33 ÷ 10) ÷ 2 = 1 65

4·95

33·00

£ 37·95

The service charge is incorrect, they have been over charged by £1 ✓

4

[Turn over

DO NOT WRITE IN THIS MARGIN

Marks | KU | RE

7. In a True or False game, players score +3 for a correct answer and –1 for a wrong answer.

THE TRUE OR FALSE GAME

Score

+3 for a correct answer
–1 for a wrong answer

(*a*) Ann had 2 questions correct and 8 wrong.

What was her score?

+3 x 2 = 6   –1 x 8 = –8

6 – 8 = –2

2

(*b*) David answered 10 questions.

His score was 18.

How many questions did he answer correctly?

10 questions
+3 - correct
-1 - wrong

7 questions were correct

2

DO NOT WRITE IN THIS MARGIN

Marks | KU | RE

8. The international sizes for writing paper are shown in the list below.

All measurements are in millimetres.

A3	297	×	420
A4	210	×	297
A5	148	×	210
A6	105	×	148
A7	74	×	105
A8	52	×	74
A9	37	×	52
A10			

By inspecting the list, write down the measurements for A10 writing paper.

A10 $2\overline{)52}$ (26) × 37

A10 26 × 37

2

9. The planet Pluto is approximately 7364 million kilometres from the Sun.

Write this number in scientific notation.

7364,000 000 km

$7{\cdot}364 \times 10^9$

2

[Turn over for Question 10 on *Page ten*

DO NOT WRITE IN THIS MARGIN

Marks | KU | RE

10.

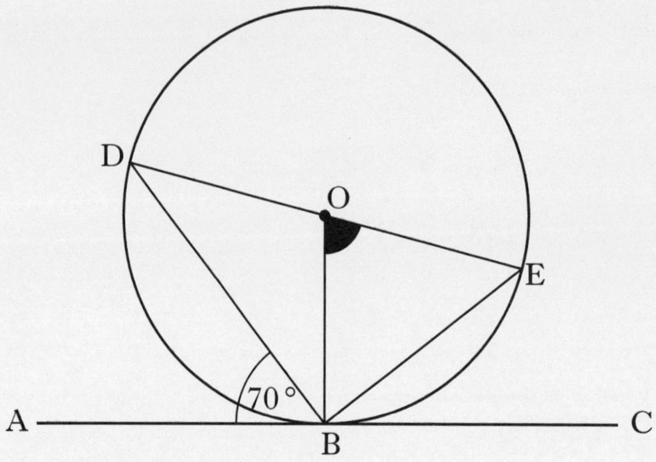

In the diagram above

- a circle, centre O, is drawn,
- the line AC is a tangent to the circle at B,
- Angle DBA = 70°.

Calculate the size of the shaded angle BOE.

40°

3

[*END OF QUESTION PAPER*]

FOR OFFICIAL USE

G

	KU	RE
Total marks		

2500/404

NATIONAL QUALIFICATIONS 2003

THURSDAY, 8 MAY
11.35 AM – 12.30 PM

MATHEMATICS STANDARD GRADE

General Level
Paper 2

Fill in these boxes and read what is printed below.

Full name of centre

Town

Forename(s)

Surname

Date of birth

Day Month Year

Scottish candidate number

Number of seat

1 **You may use a calculator.**

2 Answer as many questions as you can.

3 Write your working and answers in the spaces provided. Additional space is provided at the end of this question-answer book for use if required. If you use this space, write clearly the number of the question involved.

4 Full credit will be given only where the solution contains appropriate working.

5 Before leaving the examination room you must give this book to the invigilator. If you do not you may lose all the marks for this paper.

SCOTTISH QUALIFICATIONS AUTHORITY

FORMULAE LIST

Circumference of a circle:	$C = \pi d$
Area of a circle:	$A = \pi r^2$
Curved surface area of a cylinder:	$A = 2\pi rh$
Volume of a cylinder:	$V = \pi r^2 h$
Volume of a triangular prism:	$V = Ah$

Theorem of Pythagoras:

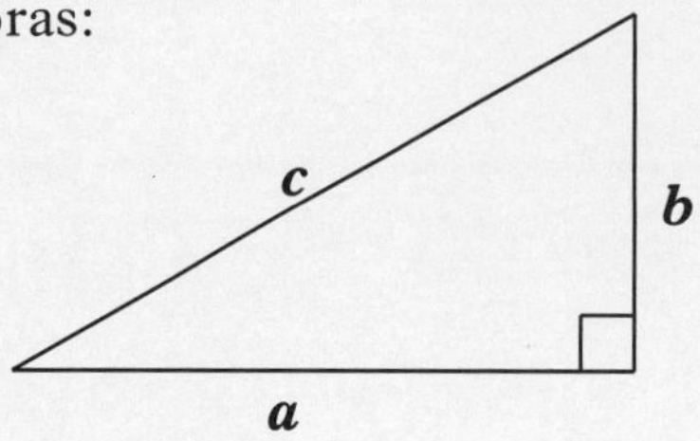

$$a^2 + b^2 = c^2$$

Trigonometric ratios in a right angled triangle:

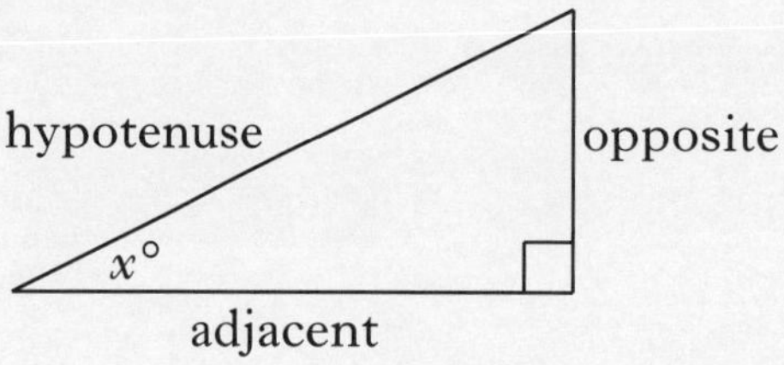

$$\tan x^\circ = \frac{\textbf{opposite}}{\textbf{adjacent}}$$

$$\sin x^\circ = \frac{\textbf{opposite}}{\textbf{hypotenuse}}$$

$$\cos x^\circ = \frac{\textbf{adjacent}}{\textbf{hypotenuse}}$$

Gradient:

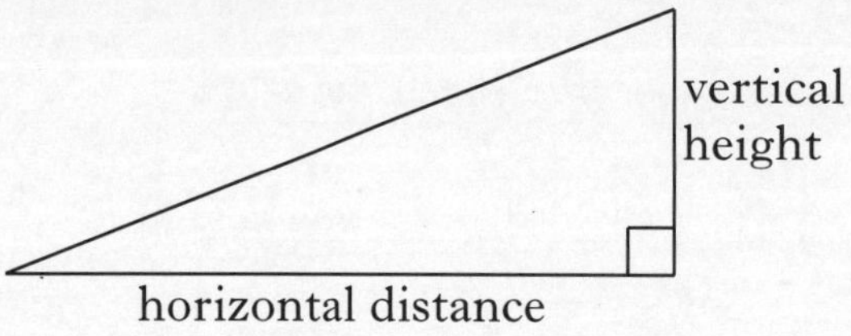

$$\textbf{Gradient} = \frac{\textbf{vertical height}}{\textbf{horizontal distance}}$$

DO NOT WRITE IN THIS MARGIN

Marks | KU | RE

1. The distance between Verona and Milan is 158 kilometres.

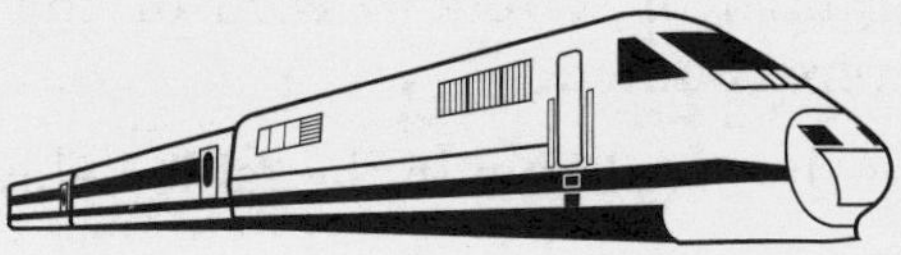

A train takes 1 hour 40 minutes to travel between these cities.

Find the average speed of the train.

S = D/T

S = 158/1.40

S = 112.86km/ph

2

2. Alice Anderson has a part-time job in a call centre.

Her basic rate of pay is £6·50 per hour.

At weekends she gets paid overtime at time and a half.

Last week she was paid £136·50, which included 4 hours overtime.

How many hours did she work at the basic rate?

3.25
2)6.50

6.50
3.25
9.75
× 4
£38.30 overtime

£136.50
38.30
£92.20

15hours
6.50)92.20

4

[Turn over

DO NOT WRITE IN THIS MARGIN

Marks | KU | RE

3. The number of letters in each of the first one hundred words of a news story were counted.

The results are shown in the table below.

Number of letters	*Frequency*	*Number of letters × frequency*
1	5	1×5 = 5
2	12	2×12 = 24
3	18	3×18 = 54
4	26	4×26 = 104
5	18	5×18 = 90
6	11	6×11 = 66
7	7	7×4 = 49
8	3	8×3 = 24
	Total = 100	Total = 416

Find the mean number of letters per word.

Give your answer correct to one decimal place.

5
24
54
104
90
66
49
24
416

416 ÷ 8 = 52

$\overline{x} = 52$

4

DO NOT WRITE IN THIS MARGIN

4. *Marks* | KU | RE

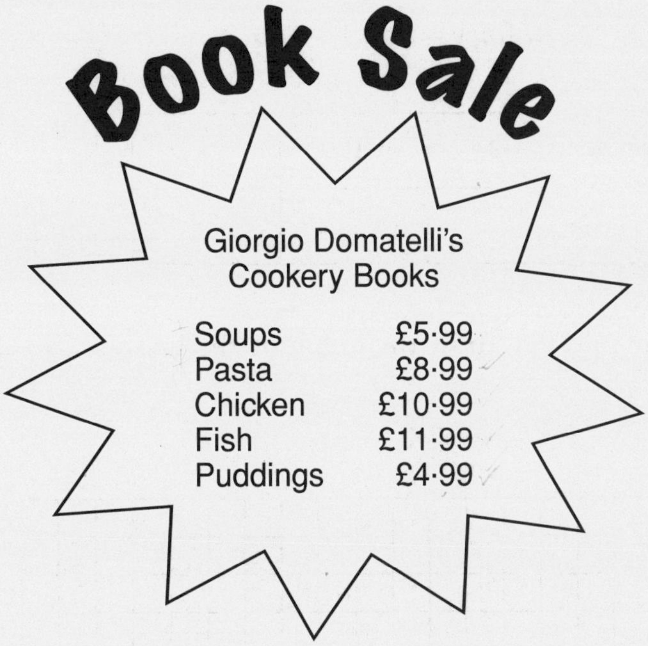

Dayna wants to buy cookery books.

She chooses books from the cookery series shown above.

- She wants to spend between £15 and £20.
- She does not buy more than one copy of any book.

One way Dayna can choose her books is shown in the table below.

Complete the table to show all the different ways Dayna can choose her books.

BOOK TITLE	BOOK TITLE	BOOK TITLE	TOTAL COST (£)
Pasta	Chicken		19·98
Fish	Soups		17.98
Pasta	Soups	Puddings	19.97
Chicken	Puddings		15.98
Puddings	Fish		16.98
Chicken	Soup		16.98

3

[Turn over

DO NOT WRITE IN THIS MARGIN

	Marks	KU	RE

5. (*a*) Complete the table below for $y = 2x - 1$.

x	−4	0	4
y	-9	-1	7

2

(*b*) Using the table in part (*a*), draw the graph of the line $y = 2x - 1$ on the grid below.

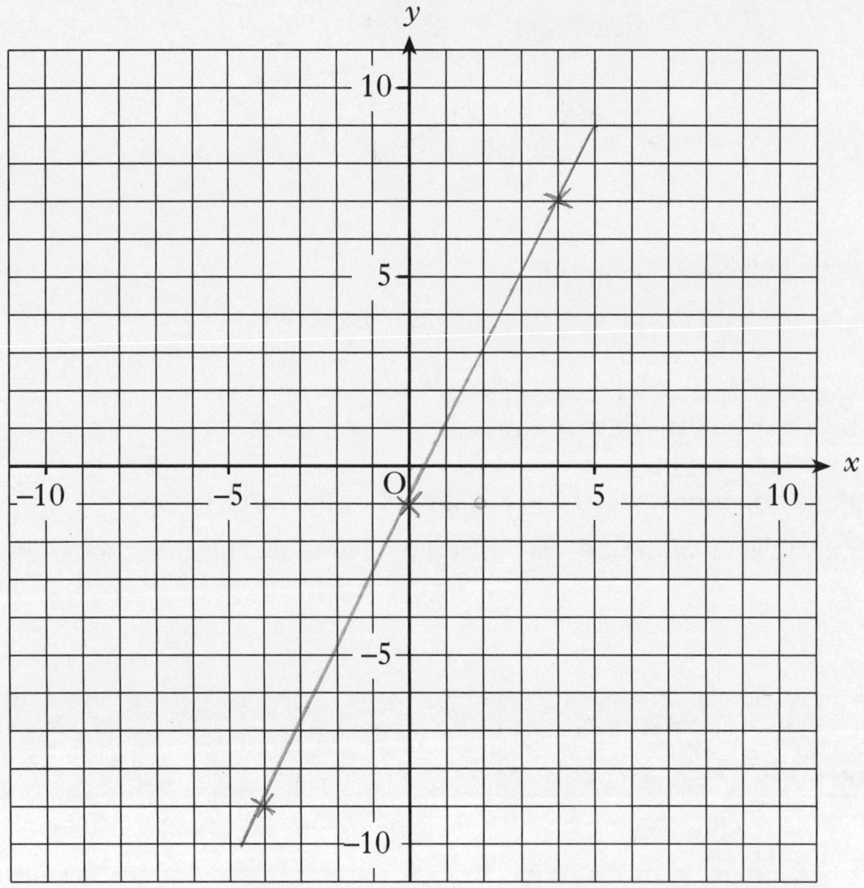

2

y = 2x − 1
y = 2(-4) − 1
y = -8 − 1
y = -9

y = 2x − 1
y = 2(-1) − 1
y = -2 − 1
y = −1

y = 2x − 1
y = 2(4) − 1
y = 8 − 1
y = 7

DO NOT WRITE IN THIS MARGIN

Marks KU RE

6.

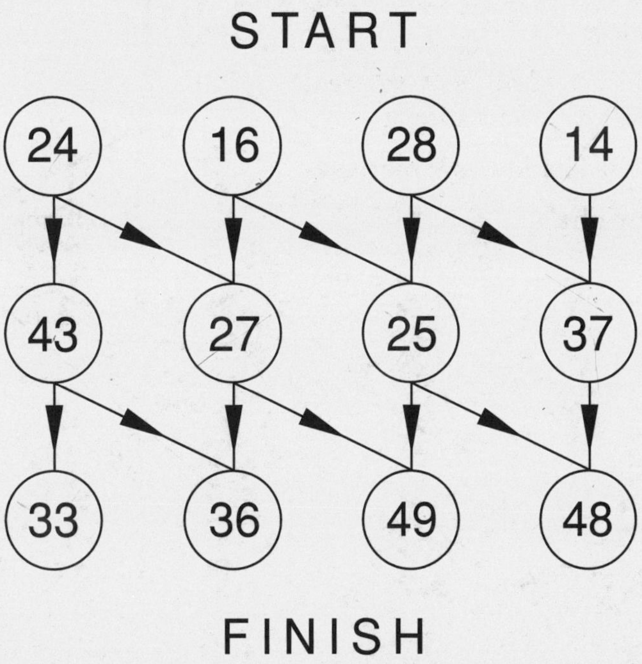

Following the arrows, use the instructions below.

Find the path which

- starts with a multiple of 4,
- moves to a prime number,
- finishes with a square number.

Write your numbers in the boxes below.

First number	Second number	Third number
24	43	36

3

[Turn over

DO NOT WRITE IN THIS MARGIN

Marks | KU | RE

7. The diagram shows the goal in American Football and its shadow.

The post below the crossbar is 3 metres high and casts a shadow 4 metres long.

The total length of the shadow is 9 metres.

Find the total goal height.

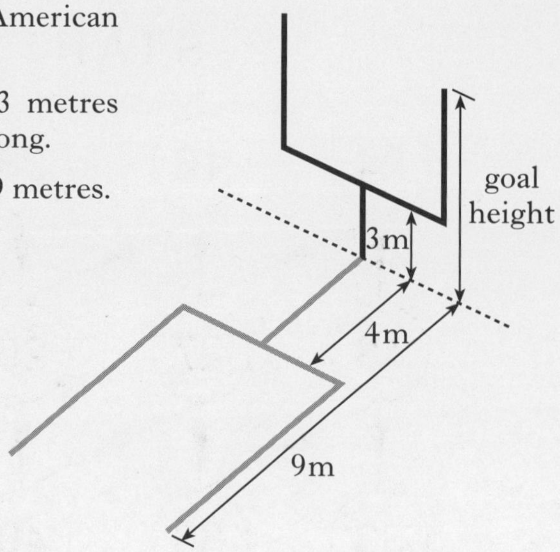

3

DO NOT WRITE IN THIS MARGIN

Marks | KU | RE

8. Alison has started a small business making wax candles.

She makes only one size of candle and it is in the shape of a cuboid.

The base of the candle is a square of side 6 centimetres.

The height of the candle is 15 centimetres.

Alison buys her wax in 10 litre tubs.

How many candles can she make from a tub of wax?

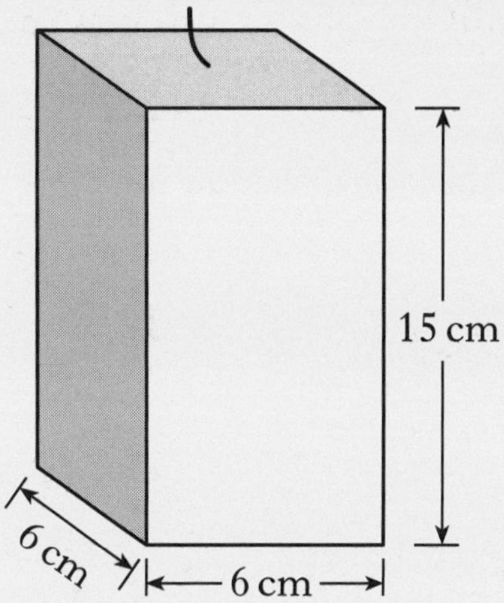

4

[Turn over

DO NOT WRITE IN THIS MARGIN

Marks | KU | RE

9. (*a*) Multiply out the brackets and collect like terms

$$3(2w + 1) + 2(8 - w).$$

6w + 3 + 16 − w
6w + w + 16 − 3
7w + 13

3

(*b*) Solve the inequality

$$3x - 4 < 11.$$

3x < 11 + 4
3x < 15
x <

2

10. The cost, *c* pounds, of a carpet varies directly as its length, *l* metres.

A carpet of length 5 metres costs £340.

(*a*) What will a carpet of length 8 metres cost?

1 metre costs
C ∝ L
C = k × L
C = 5k
£340 = 5k
$\frac{340}{5}$ = k
£68 = k

8 × £68
8 metres = £544

3

(*b*) What length is a carpet which costs £238?

238 ÷ 68
3.5 metres = £238

2

DO NOT WRITE IN THIS MARGIN

Marks | KU | RE

11. An adventure park is installing a climbing wall.

The wall is in the shape of a cylinder to which climbing pegs are attached.

The radius of the cylinder is 1·5 metres.

The cylinder has a curved surface area of 75·5 square metres.

What height will the cylinder be?

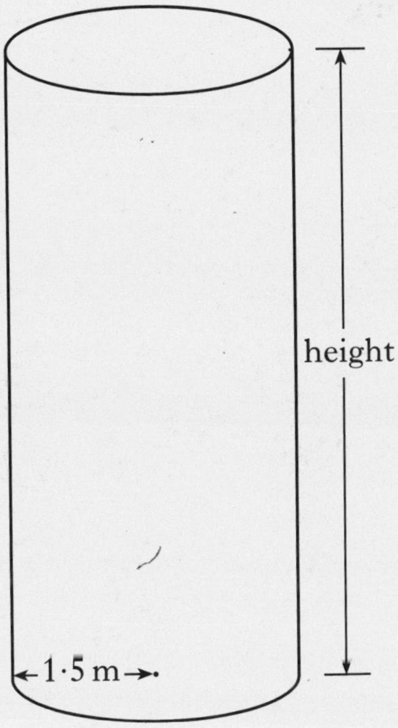

4

[Turn over

DO NOT WRITE IN THIS MARGIN

Marks | KU | RE

12.

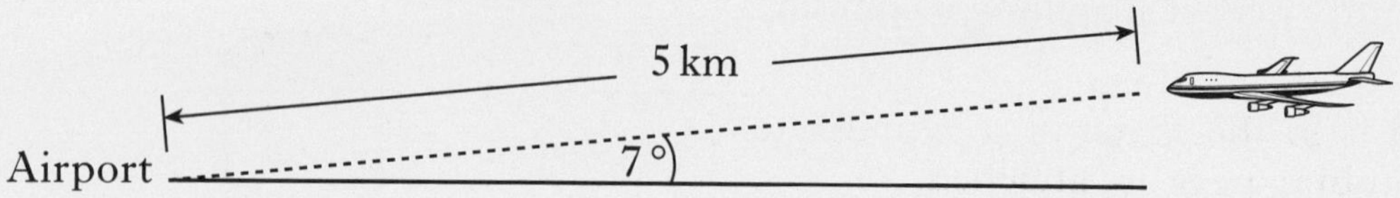

An aircraft is approaching Glasgow airport.

The angle of elevation of the aircraft from the airport is 7°.

The aircraft is at a distance of 5 km from the airport.

Find the height of the aircraft, to the nearest metre.

Do not use a scale drawing.

4

DO NOT WRITE IN THIS MARGIN

Marks | KU | RE

13. A large advertising banner is hanging from a building.

The banner is an isosceles triangle.

The top edge of the banner is 20 metres long and each of the other two sides is 26 metres long.

Find the area of the banner.

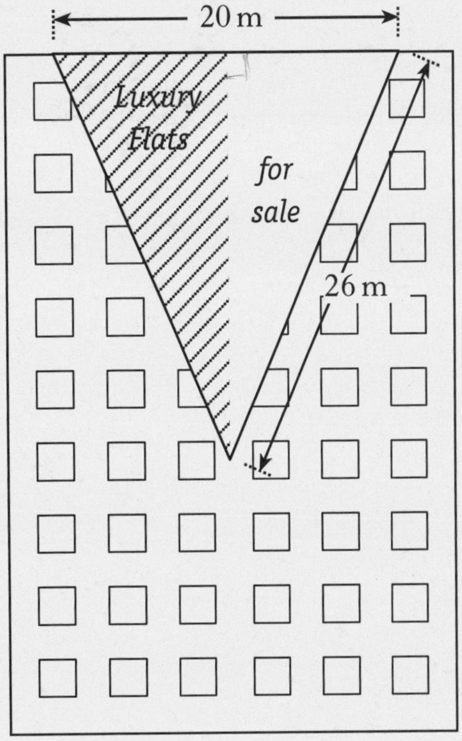

$A = l \times b \frac{1}{2}$

$A = \frac{1}{2} \times 26 \times 20$

$A = 520 \times \frac{1}{2}$

$A = 260\ m^2$

4

[*END OF QUESTION PAPER*]

[BLANK PAGE]

2004 | General

[BLANK PAGE]

FOR OFFICIAL USE

G

	KU	RE
Total marks		

2500/403

NATIONAL QUALIFICATIONS 2004

FRIDAY, 7 MAY
10.40 AM – 11.15 AM

MATHEMATICS STANDARD GRADE

General Level
Paper 1
Non-calculator

Fill in these boxes and read what is printed below.

Full name of centre

Town

Forename(s)

Surname

Date of birth

Day Month Year

Scottish candidate number

Number of seat

1 **You may not use a calculator.**

2 Answer as many questions as you can.

3 Write your working and answers in the spaces provided. Additional space is provided at the end of this question-answer book for use if required. If you use this space, write clearly the number of the question involved.

4 Full credit will be given only where the solution contains appropriate working.

5 Before leaving the examination room you must give this book to the invigilator. If you do not you may lose all the marks for this paper.

SCOTTISH QUALIFICATIONS AUTHORITY

FORMULAE LIST

Circumference of a circle:	$C = \pi d$
Area of a circle:	$A = \pi r^2$
Curved surface area of a cylinder:	$A = 2\pi rh$
Volume of a cylinder:	$V = \pi r^2 h$
Volume of a triangular prism:	$V = Ah$

Theorem of Pythagoras:

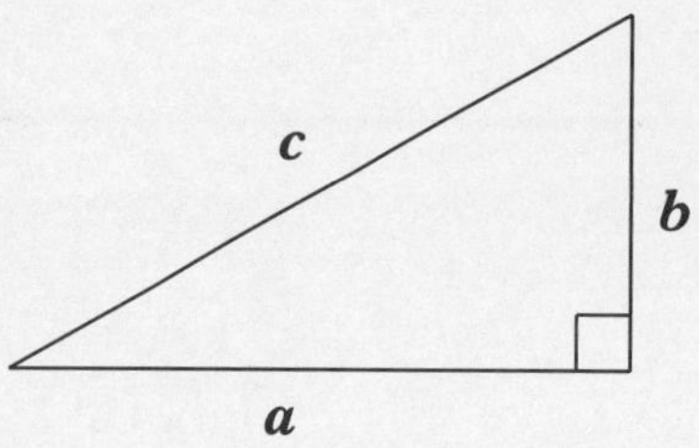

$$a^2 + b^2 = c^2$$

Trigonometric ratios in a right angled triangle:

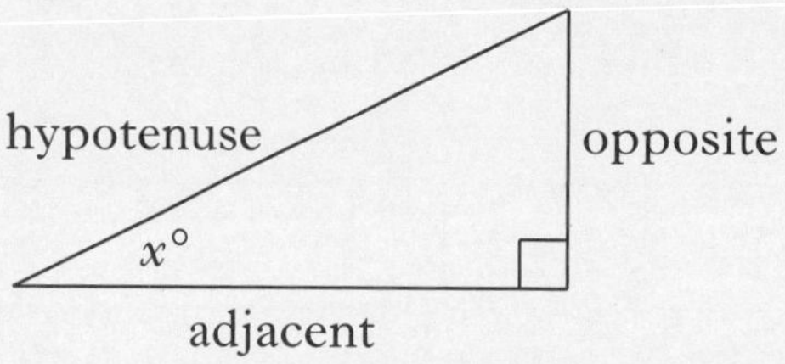

$$\tan x^\circ = \frac{\text{opposite}}{\text{adjacent}}$$

$$\sin x^\circ = \frac{\text{opposite}}{\text{hypotenuse}}$$

$$\cos x^\circ = \frac{\text{adjacent}}{\text{hypotenuse}}$$

Gradient:

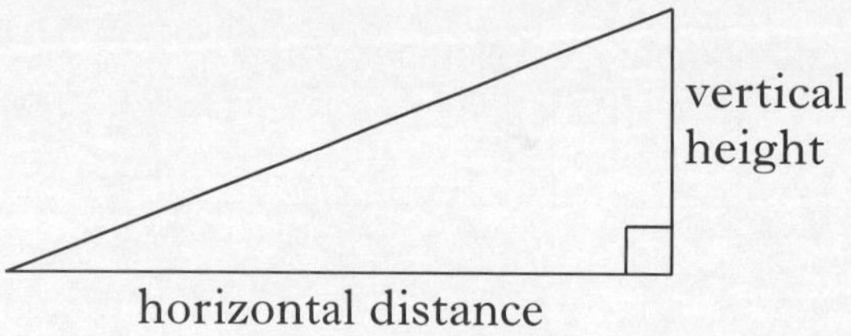

$$\text{Gradient} = \frac{\text{vertical height}}{\text{horizontal distance}}$$

DO NOT WRITE IN THIS MARGIN

Marks | KU | RE

1. Carry out the following calculations.

(*a*) 14·93 – 3·7 + 2·15

3.7
+ 2.15
5·85

14.93
-5.85
9·08

9.08

1

(*b*) 42·8 × 7

42.8
× 7
299.6

1

(*c*) 1710 ÷ 3000

0·57
3000) 1710

1

(*d*) 90% of £180

18.
10) 180

18
×9
£162

90% of £180 = £162

2

2. Express $\frac{3}{7}$ as a decimal.

Give your answer correct to two decimal places.

2

DO NOT WRITE IN THIS MARGIN

Marks | KU | RE

3. Ann Fiona Johnstone has drawn a design which uses her initials.

She wants her finished design to be symmetrical.

Complete her design so that the dotted line is an axis of symmetry.

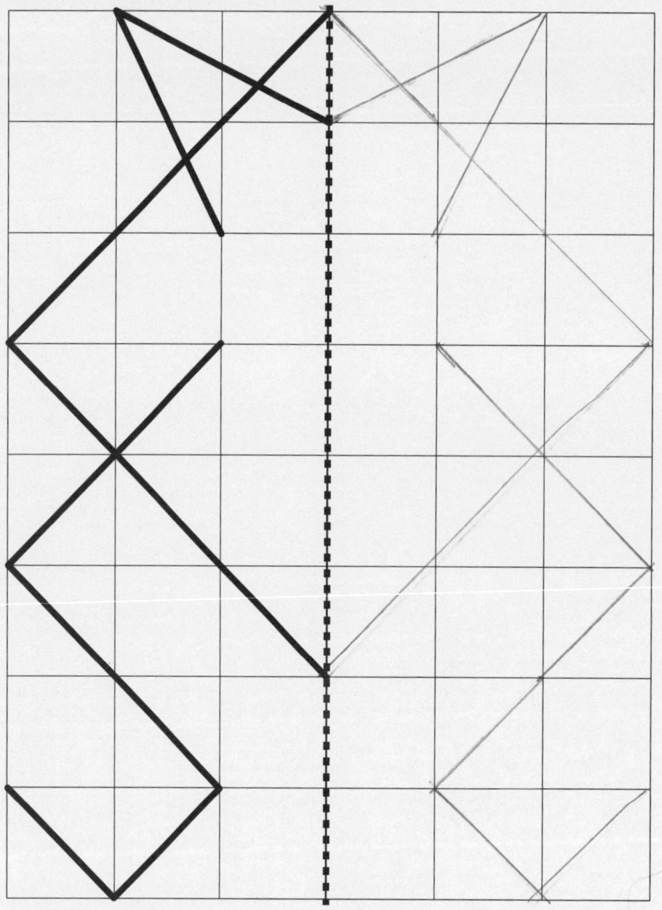

3

4. The largest ocean in the world is the Pacific Ocean.

Its area is approximately $1 \cdot 813 \times 10^8$ square kilometres.

Write this number in full.

181300000 km²

1

DO NOT WRITE IN THIS MARGIN

Marks | KU | RE

5. A patient in hospital had his temperature checked every two hours.

The results are shown in the table below.

Time	12 noon	2 pm	4 pm	6 pm	8 pm	10 pm
Temperature (° C)	38·2	38·6	38·1	37·9	37·5	36·9

Illustrate this data on the grid below using a line graph.

Temperature Chart

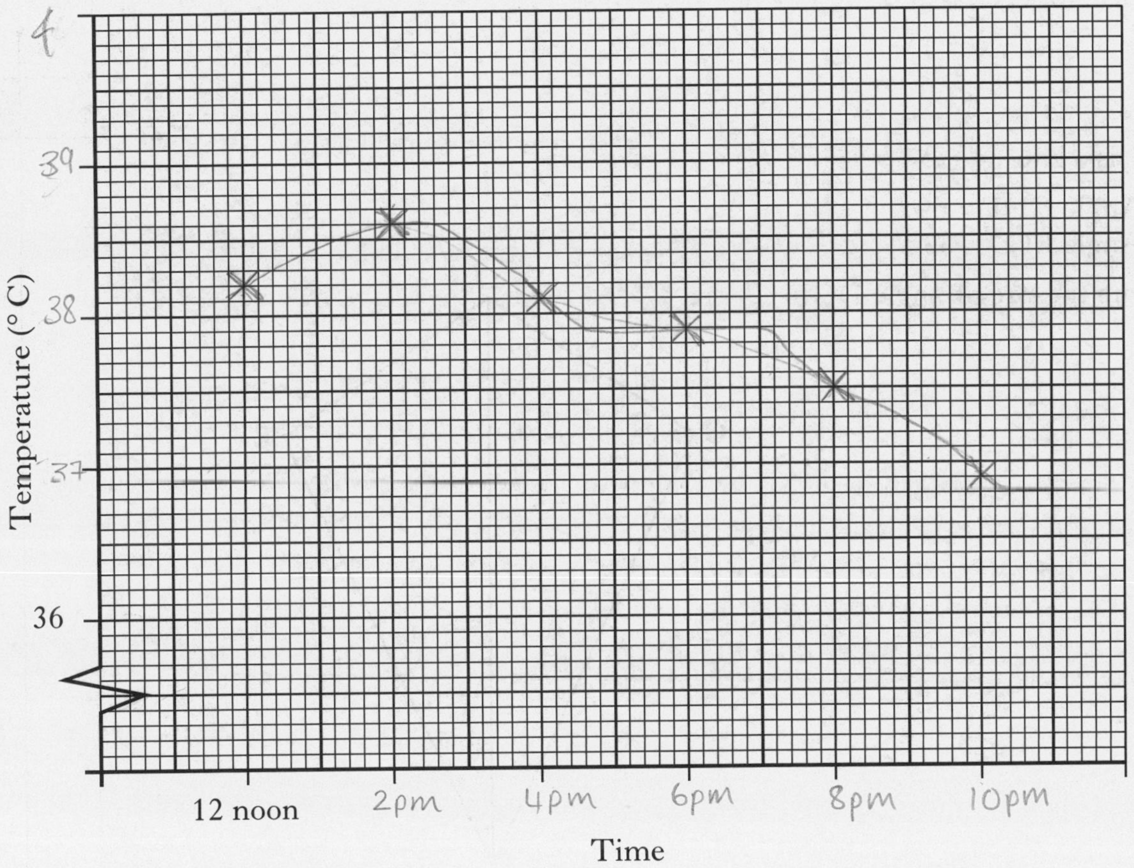

4

[Turn over

DO NOT WRITE IN THIS MARGIN

Marks | KU | RE

6. Last month a garage sold 12 red cars, 9 silver cars and 15 black cars.

Joe bought one of these cars.

What is the probability that the car Joe bought was silver?

Give your answer as a fraction in its simplest form.

9
12
15
36

9/36 $\frac{1}{4}$

2

7. DEFG is a kite.

- Angle GDF = 69 °
- Angle EFD = 33 °

Calculate the size of angle DGF.

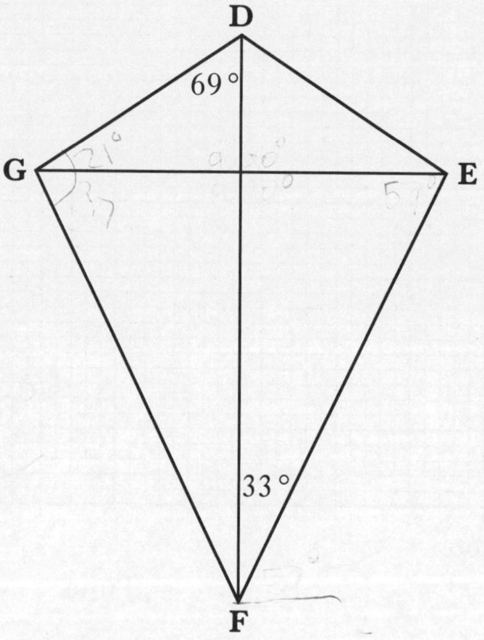

3

DO NOT WRITE IN THIS MARGIN

Marks | KU | RE

8. Christy needs a four-digit code to switch on her mobile phone.

She uses the digits from her birth date 4/3/89, but in a different order.

She knows that the last digit is 8.

One of the possible four-digit codes Christy could try is shown in the table below.

Complete the table to show all the possible four-digit codes.

4	3	9	8
4	9	3	8
9	3	4	8
9	4	3	8
3	9	4	8
3	4	9	8

3

9. A recipe for Shortbread uses the following ingredients.

300 grams flour
100 grams sugar
200 grams butter

Alana has only 240 grams of flour.

To make Shortbread using all of the 240 grams of flour she will have to adjust the quantities of sugar and butter.

How many grams of sugar and how many grams of butter should she use?

4

DO NOT WRITE IN THIS MARGIN

Marks | KU | RE

10. The heating in Bruce's house switches on automatically when the outside temperature drops to –5 °C.

One day last winter the outside temperature was 3 °C.

Calculate the drop in temperature when the heating switched on automatically.

−5 + 3 = 8°C

2

11. Andrew and his brother are flying to America on holiday.

Their flight times are shown below.

Depart Glasgow	30/6/04	2120
Arrive Reykjavik, Iceland	30/6/04	2235
Depart Reykjavik, Iceland	1/7/04	0105
Arrive New York, USA	1/7/04	0455

How long will the brothers have to wait at Reykjavik in Iceland before their flight to New York?

$2\frac{1}{2}$ hours

2

[*END OF QUESTION PAPER*]

FOR OFFICIAL USE

G

	KU	RE
Total marks		

2500/404

NATIONAL QUALIFICATIONS 2004

FRIDAY, 7 MAY
11.35 AM – 12.30 PM

MATHEMATICS STANDARD GRADE
General Level
Paper 2

Fill in these boxes and read what is printed below.

Full name of centre

Town

Forename(s)

Surname

Date of birth

Day Month Year

Scottish candidate number

Number of seat

1 **You may use a calculator.**

2 Answer as many questions as you can.

3 Write your working and answers in the spaces provided. Additional space is provided at the end of this question-answer book for use if required. If you use this space, write clearly the number of the question involved.

4 Full credit will be given only where the solution contains appropriate working.

5 Before leaving the examination room you must give this book to the invigilator. If you do not you may lose all the marks for this paper.

FORMULAE LIST

Circumference of a circle:	$C = \pi d$
Area of a circle:	$A = \pi r^2$
Curved surface area of a cylinder:	$A = 2\pi rh$
Volume of a cylinder:	$V = \pi r^2 h$
Volume of a triangular prism:	$V = Ah$

Theorem of Pythagoras:

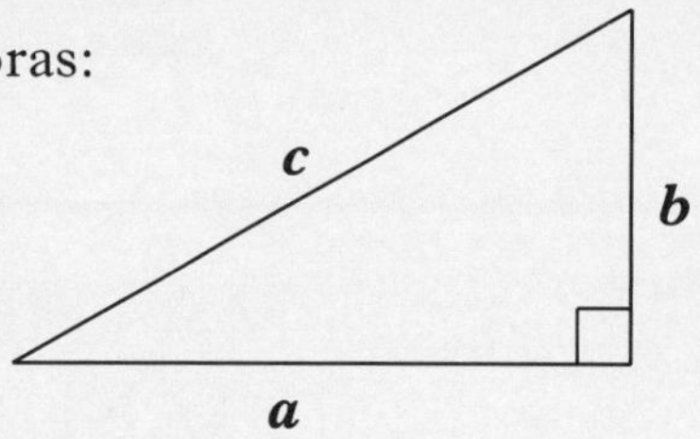

$$a^2 + b^2 = c^2$$

Trigonometric ratios in a right angled triangle:

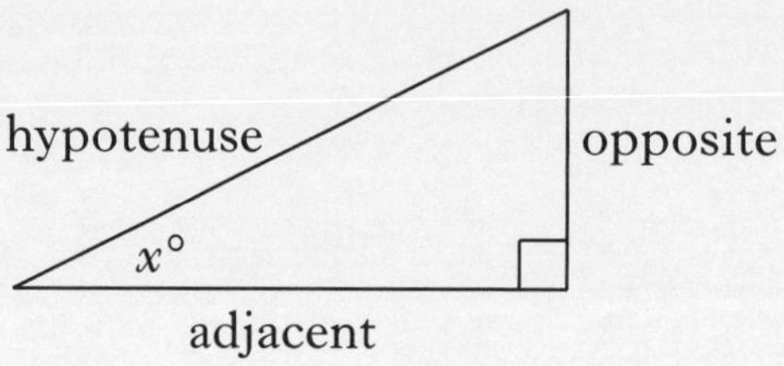

$$\tan x^\circ = \frac{\textbf{opposite}}{\textbf{adjacent}}$$

$$\sin x^\circ = \frac{\textbf{opposite}}{\textbf{hypotenuse}}$$

$$\cos x^\circ = \frac{\textbf{adjacent}}{\textbf{hypotenuse}}$$

Gradient:

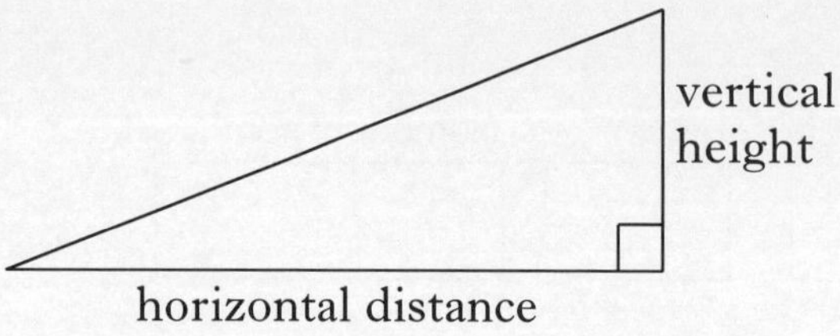

$$\textbf{Gradient} = \frac{\textbf{vertical height}}{\textbf{horizontal distance}}$$

DO NOT WRITE IN THIS MARGIN

Marks | KU | RE

1. 100 grams of wholemeal bread contain the following:

Protein	10 grams
Carbohydrates	55 grams
Fibre	9 grams
Fat	3 grams
Other	23 grams

A pie chart is to be drawn to show this information.

What size of angle should be used for the carbohydrates?

DO NOT DRAW A PIE CHART.

3.6
100 ⟌ 360

3.6
× 55
198°

2

[Turn over

DO NOT WRITE IN THIS MARGIN

Marks | KU | RE

2. A company manufactures boxes of tacks and claims that there are "on average" 60 tacks per box.

This claim is tested by counting the number of tacks in a sample of 100 boxes.

The results are shown below.

Number of tacks	Frequency	Number of tacks × Frequency
57	7	57×7 = 399
58	13	58×13 = 754
59	21	59×21 = 1239
60	24	60×24 = 1440
61	19	61×19 = 1159
62	12	62×12 = 744
63	4	63×4 = 252
Totals	100	

(*a*) Find the mean number of tacks per box.

399
754
1239
1440
1159
744
252
5987

5987 ÷ 7 = 855.29

3

(*b*) Is the company's claim reasonable?

You must give a reason for your answer.

Yes with reason.

1

DO NOT WRITE IN THIS MARGIN

Marks KU RE

3. The sketch below shows the net of a three-dimensional shape.

The net consists of a rectangle and two equal circles of radius 3 centimetres.

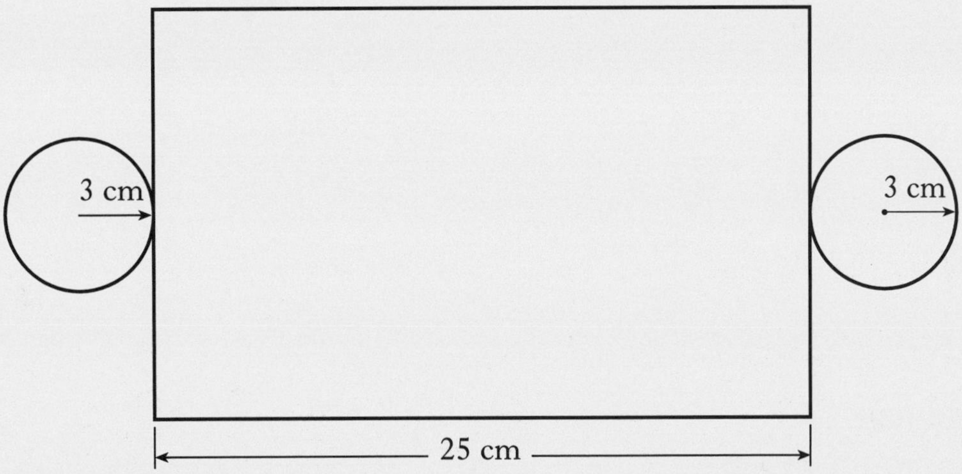

Find the **volume** of the three-dimensional shape formed from this net.

3

[Turn over

DO NOT WRITE IN THIS MARGIN

Marks | KU | RE

4. (*a*) Solve algebraically

$$5x - 2 = 2x + 19.$$

$5x - 2x = 19 + 2$

$3x = 21$

$x = 7$

3

(*b*) Factorise fully

$$12 + 8p.$$

$4(3 + 2p)$

2

DO NOT WRITE IN THIS MARGIN

Marks | KU | RE

5.

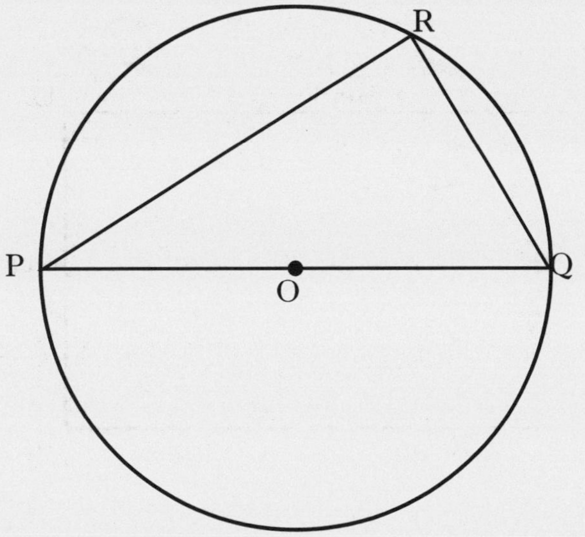

PQ is a diameter of the circle with centre O.

R is a point on the circumference of the circle.

PR is 12 centimetres.

RQ is 5·5 centimetres.

Calculate the length of the radius of the circle. **4**

[Turn over

DO NOT WRITE IN THIS MARGIN

Marks | KU | RE

6.

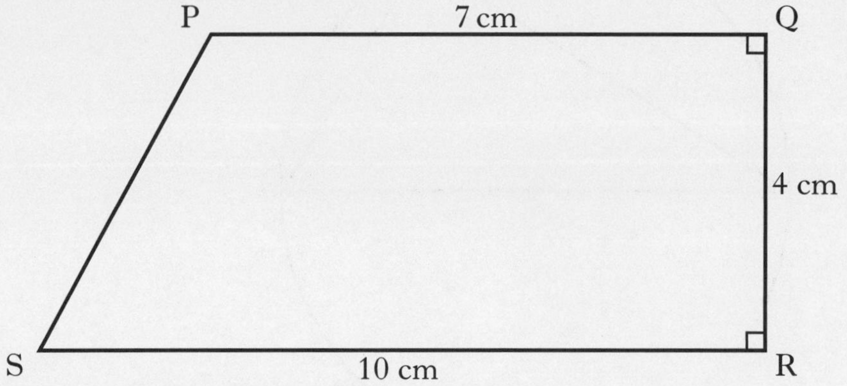

PQRS is a trapezium.

- PQ = 7 centimetres.
- QR = 4 centimetres.
- SR = 10 centimetres.
- Angles PQR and QRS are both right angles.

Calculate the size of angle PSR.

Do not use a scale drawing.

4

DO NOT WRITE IN THIS MARGIN

Marks | KU | RE

7. (*a*) John is going to Italy on holiday.

He changes £500 to Euros.

The exchange rate is £1 = 1·51 Euros.

How many Euros will he get? **2**

(*b*) While in Italy he decides to visit Switzerland for a day.

He wants to change 100 Euros to Swiss Francs.

John knows the exchange rate is £1 = 2·33 Swiss Francs.

How many Swiss Francs should he get for 100 Euros? **3**

DO NOT WRITE IN THIS MARGIN

Marks | KU | RE

8. The floor of a conservatory consists of a rectangle and a semicircle.

The floor has the shape shown below.

The measurements are in metres.

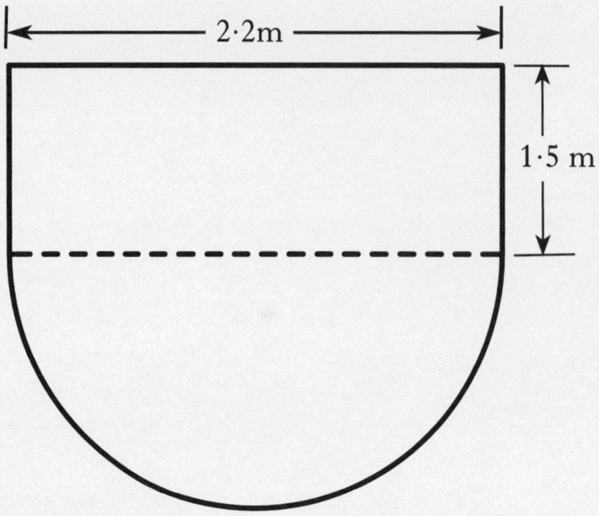

Find the total area of the floor. **4**

DO NOT WRITE IN THIS MARGIN

Marks | KU | RE

9. A basic cable television package, which includes 30 channels, costs £8·75 per month.

The cost of installation is £75 which will be included in the first month's bill.

Additional channels can be added to the basic service.

- The movie channels package costs £12·50 per month.
- The music channels package costs £7·50 per month.
- The sports channels package costs £14·50 per month.

The Mackie family's first bill after having cable television installed was £98·25.

They chose the basic cable television package plus one additional channels package.

Which additional package did they choose?

Give a reason for your answer.

3

[Turn over

DO NOT WRITE IN THIS MARGIN

Marks | KU | RE

10. Janice is planning to go on holiday to Florida.

She wants to book with FloridaSun Holidays and stay at the Parkway Hotel.

The table below shows the pricing information for the Parkway Hotel.

FloridaSun Holidays PARKWAY HOTEL	Prices are per person in £s	
No. of Nights	**7**	**14**
May 17	445	725
24	459	735
31	465	749
June 7	479	765
14	499	779
21	509	789
28	519	799
July 5	525	805
12	535	825
19	545	839
26	609	855
Aug 2	615	869
9	625	895
16	639	875
23	539	845
30	519	805

(*a*) Janice wants to stay in the Parkway Hotel for 14 nights.

What will be the price if her holiday starts on 5th July? **1**

DO NOT WRITE IN THIS MARGIN

Marks KU RE

10. (continued)

(*b*) The Parkway Hotel charges an extra £4·95 per person per night for a single room.

How much extra will Janice pay for her 14 night holiday if she wants a single room? **1**

(*c*) If Janice books today she will get a 20% discount on her **total cost**.

Find the discounted price of her 14 night holiday in a single room from 5th July. **2**

Marks | KU | RE

11. Mara travels 1850 miles every month.

Currently her car runs on unleaded petrol, which costs 76·9p per litre and her car travels 8·5 miles per litre.

(*a*) What is her monthly petrol bill? **2**

Mara is thinking of having her car converted to run on Liquid Petroleum Gas (LPG).

LPG costs 38·9p per litre and using this fuel her car will travel 7·8 miles per litre.

(*b*) What will be her monthly saving if she converts her car to run on LPG? **2**

DO NOT WRITE IN THIS MARGIN

Marks | KU | RE

11. (continued)

(*c*) The cost of converting Mara's car to run on LPG is £800.

How many months of savings will it take to recover the cost of the conversion? **2**

[Turn over

DO NOT WRITE IN THIS MARGIN

Marks | KU | RE

12. The current, C amps, of an electrical appliance is calculated using the formula

$$C = \frac{P}{240}, \text{ where } P \text{ watts is the power rating.}$$

- A hairdryer has a power rating of 850 watts.
- The fuse used should be the one just bigger than the calculated current.
- The choice of fuses is 3 amp, 5 amp and 13 amp.

Which fuse should be used?

3

DO NOT WRITE IN THIS MARGIN

Marks | KU | RE

13. The diagram below shows the position of two buoys.

Sofie has to sail her yacht between the two buoys so that it is always the same distance from each buoy.

Show the yacht's **course** on the diagram.

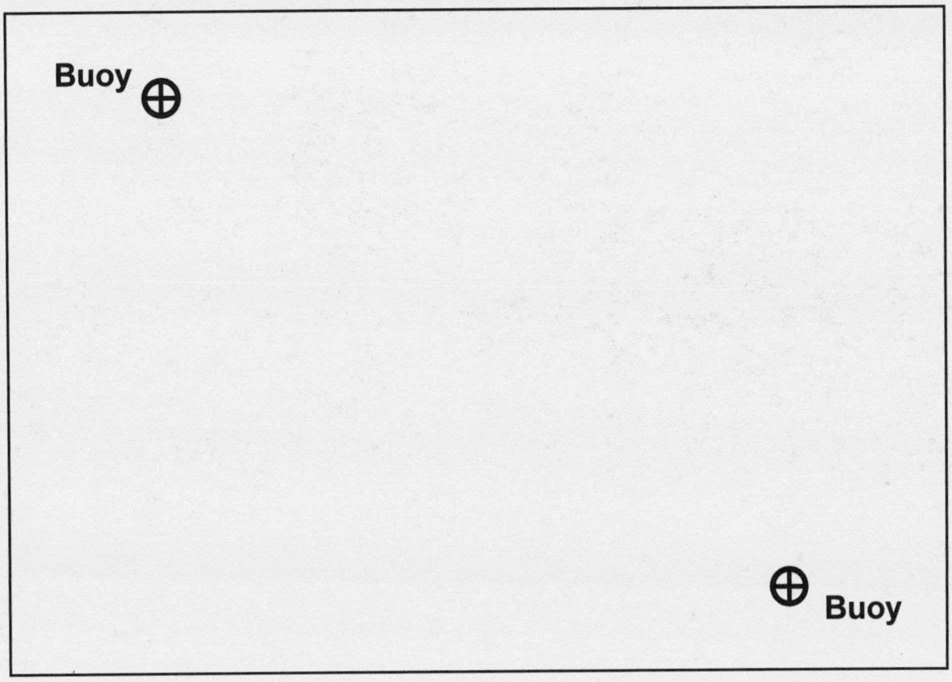

2

[*END OF QUESTION PAPER*]

ADDITIONAL SPACE FOR ANSWERS

2005 | General

[BLANK PAGE]

FOR OFFICIAL USE

G

	KU	RE
Total marks		

2500/403

NATIONAL QUALIFICATIONS 2005

FRIDAY, 6 MAY
10.40 AM – 11.15 AM

MATHEMATICS STANDARD GRADE

General Level
Paper 1
Non-calculator

Fill in these boxes and read what is printed below.

Full name of centre

Town

Forename(s)

Surname

Date of birth
Day Month Year

Scottish candidate number

Number of seat

1 **You may not use a calculator.**

2 Answer as many questions as you can.

3 Write your working and answers in the spaces provided. Additional space is provided at the end of this question-answer book for use if required. If you use this space, write clearly the number of the question involved.

4 Full credit will be given only where the solution contains appropriate working.

5 Before leaving the examination room you must give this book to the invigilator. If you do not you may lose all the marks for this paper.

SCOTTISH QUALIFICATIONS AUTHORITY

LIB 2500/403 6/65470

FORMULAE LIST

Circumference of a circle: $C = \pi d$

Area of a circle: $A = \pi r^2$

Curved surface area of a cylinder: $A = 2\pi rh$

Volume of a cylinder: $V = \pi r^2 h$

Volume of a triangular prism: $V = Ah$

Theorem of Pythagoras:

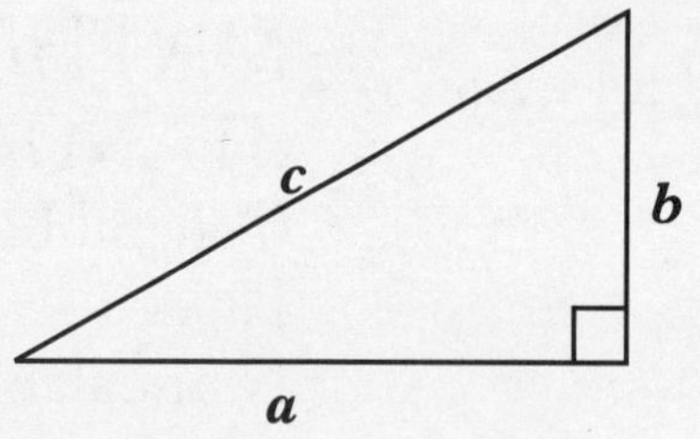

$$a^2 + b^2 = c^2$$

Trigonometric ratios
in a right angled
triangle:

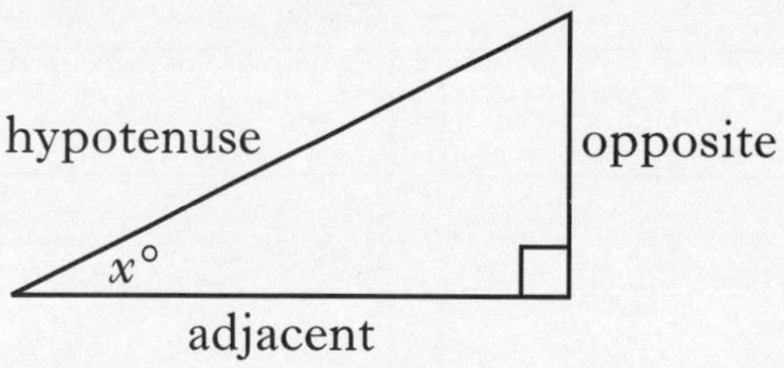

$$\tan x^\circ = \frac{\text{opposite}}{\text{adjacent}}$$

$$\sin x^\circ = \frac{\text{opposite}}{\text{hypotenuse}}$$

$$\cos x^\circ = \frac{\text{adjacent}}{\text{hypotenuse}}$$

Gradient:

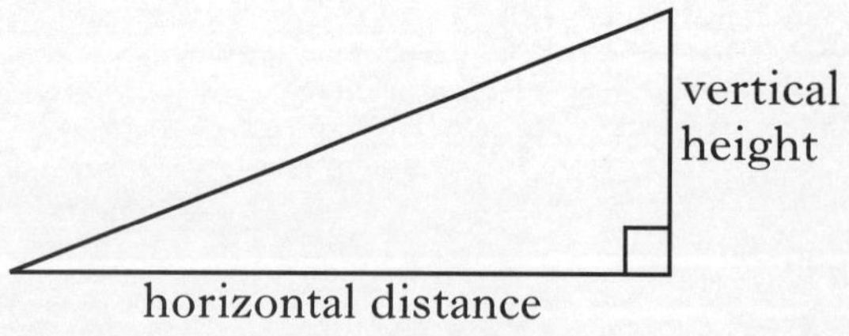

$$\text{Gradient} = \frac{\text{vertical height}}{\text{horizontal distance}}$$

DO NOT WRITE IN THIS MARGIN

Marks | KU | RE

1. Carry out the following calculations.

(*a*) 209·3 − 175·48

209.80
−175.48
33.82

1

(*b*) 56·7 × 90

56.7
×90
000.00
510.3
510.3

1

(*c*) 324·1 ÷ 7

047.3
7) 324.1
47.3

1

(*d*) $\frac{3}{4}$ of 56 cm

14
4) 56

14
×3
42

42

2

2. When an aircraft leaves Prestwick airport the outside temperature is 12 ° Celsius.

The aircraft climbs to 10 000 metres and the outside temperature is –50 ° Celsius.

Find the difference between these temperatures.

50
+12
62°C

2

DO NOT WRITE IN THIS MARGIN

Marks | KU | RE

3. Sandra is working on the design for a bracelet.

She is using matches to make each shape.

Shape 1 **Shape 2** **Shape 3** **Shape 4**

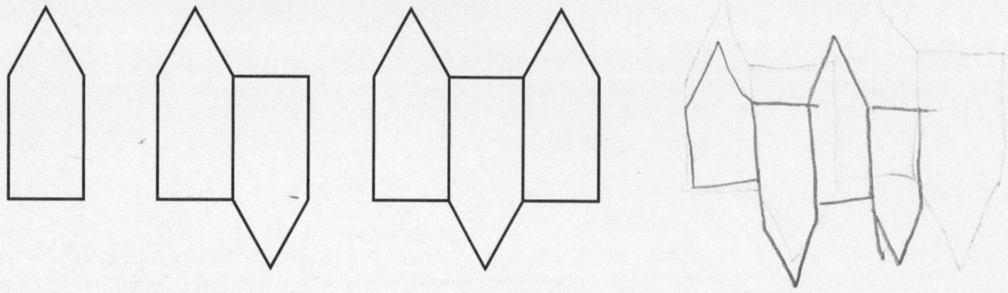

(*a*) Draw shape 4. **1**

(*b*) Complete the following table.

Shape number (s)	1	2	3	4	5	6	10	13
Number of matches (m)	5	9	13	17	21	25	41	53

2

(*c*) Find a formula for calculating the number of matches, (m), when you know the shape number, (s).

$m = 4s + 1$

2

(*d*) Which shape number uses 61 matches?

You must show your working.

$61 - 1 = 60$

$60 \div 4 = 15$

Shape 15 uses 60 matches

2

DO NOT WRITE IN THIS MARGIN

Marks | KU | RE

4. A ship is transporting 2800 cars.

Each car is worth £20 000.

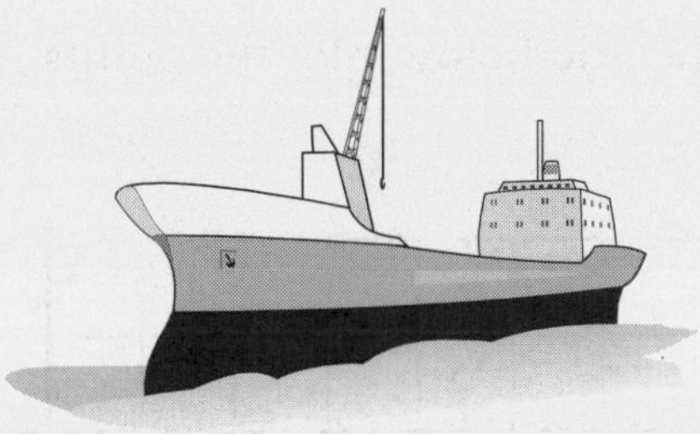

(*a*) What is the total value of all the cars?

2800
×20000

28
×200
560 × 100

56000000

1

(*b*) Write the total value in scientific notation.

5·7 × 10⁷

1

[Turn over

DO NOT WRITE IN THIS MARGIN

Marks | KU | RE

5. (*a*) On the grid below, plot the points A(7, 5), B(5, –1) and C(–1, –3).

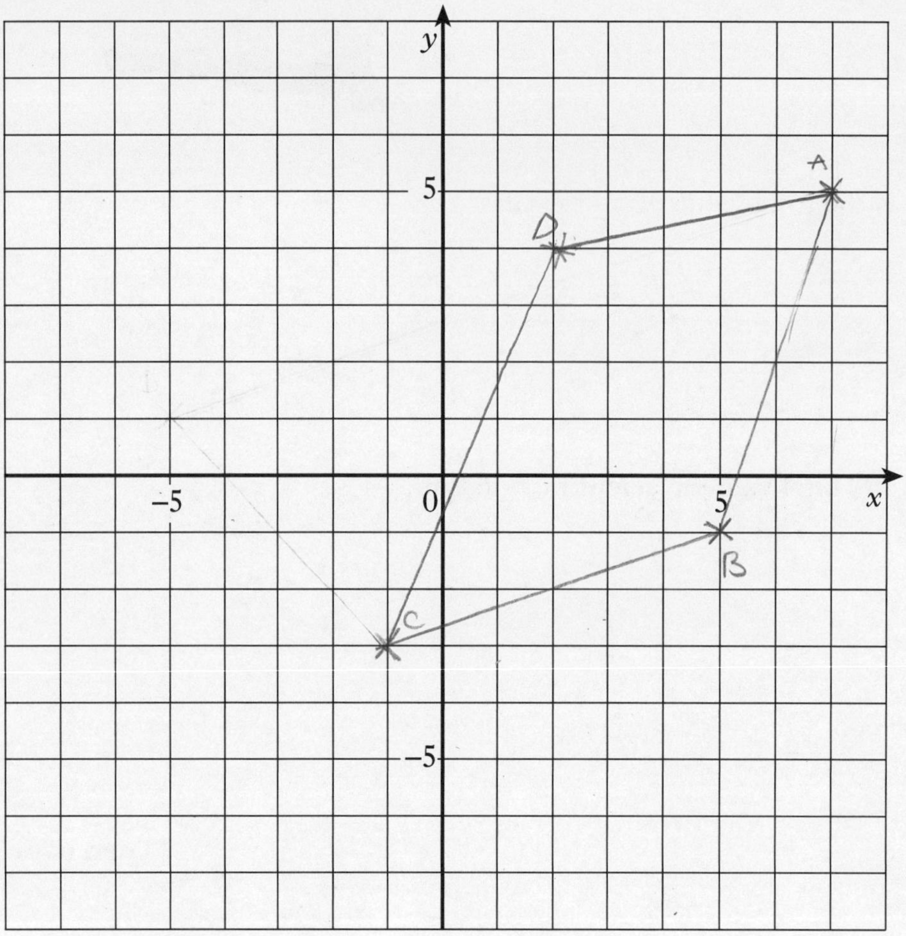

2

(*b*) Plot a fourth point D so that ABCD is a rhombus. 1

(*c*) Reflect rhombus ABCD in the ***y*-axis**. 2

DO NOT WRITE IN THIS MARGIN

Marks | KU | RE

6. The table below can be used to convert tyre pressures from pounds per square inch (lb/sq in) to kilograms per square centimetre (kg/sq cm).

lb/sq in	20	22	24	26	28	30	32	34
kg/sq cm	1·41	1·55	1·69	1·83	1·97	2·11	2·25	2·39

Convert **29 lb/sq in** to **kg/sq cm**.

2·04 kg/sqcm

1·97 + 0·07 = 2·04

2·11 − 1·97 = ·14

2

7. (*a*) Graham goes into a shop and buys a bottle of water and a cheese roll for £1·38.

In the same shop, Alan pays £1·77 for 2 bottles of water and a cheese roll.

How much does a bottle of water cost?

39p

1

(*b*) Craig goes into the shop and buys 4 bottles of water and 3 cheese rolls.

How much will this cost?

39 × 4 = 1·56

99 × 3 = 2·97

2·97 + 1·56 = £4·53

3

[Turn over

DO NOT WRITE IN THIS MARGIN

Marks | KU | RE

8. John buys a football programme for £1·60 and sells it for £2·00.

Calculate his percentage profit.

3

9.

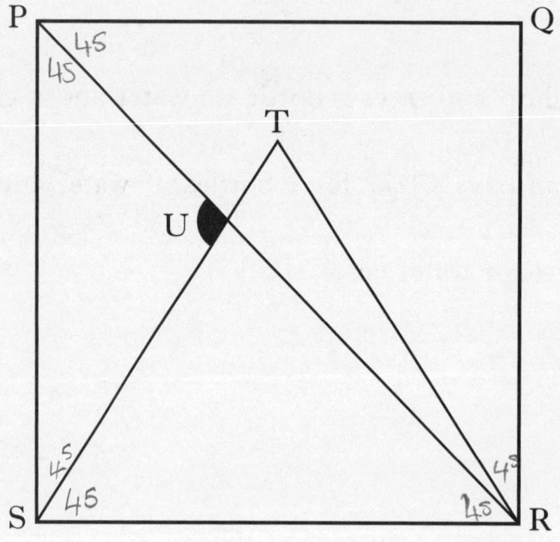

In the diagram above

- PQRS is a square
- PR is a diagonal of the square
- Triangle RST is equilateral.

Calculate the size of the shaded angle SUP.

3

[*END OF QUESTION PAPER*]

FOR OFFICIAL USE

G

	KU	RE
Total marks		

2500/404

NATIONAL
QUALIFICATIONS
2005

FRIDAY, 6 MAY
11.35 AM – 12.30 PM

MATHEMATICS
STANDARD GRADE
General Level
Paper 2

Fill in these boxes and read what is printed below.

Full name of centre

Town

Forename(s)

Surname

Date of birth
Day Month Year

Scottish candidate number

Number of seat

1 **You may use a calculator.**

2 Answer as many questions as you can.

3 Write your working and answers in the spaces provided. Additional space is provided at the end of this question-answer book for use if required. If you use this space, write clearly the number of the question involved.

4 Full credit will be given only where the solution contains appropriate working.

5 Before leaving the examination room you must give this book to the invigilator. If you do not you may lose all the marks for this paper.

SCOTTISH
QUALIFICATIONS
AUTHORITY

FORMULAE LIST

Circumference of a circle:	$C = \pi d$
Area of a circle:	$A = \pi r^2$
Curved surface area of a cylinder:	$A = 2\pi rh$
Volume of a cylinder:	$V = \pi r^2 h$
Volume of a triangular prism:	$V = Ah$

Theorem of Pythagoras:

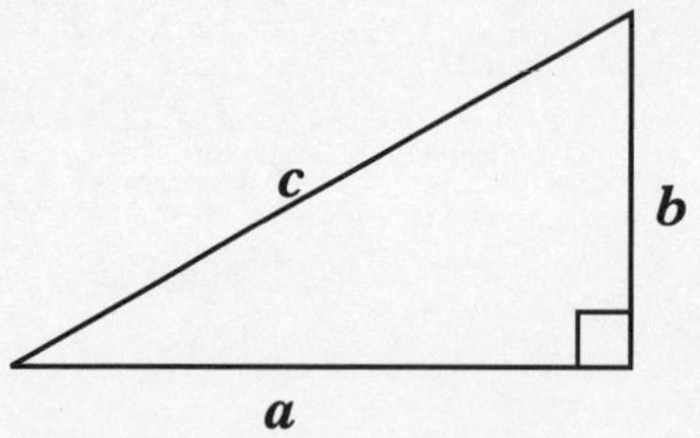

$$a^2 + b^2 = c^2$$

Trigonometric ratios in a right angled triangle:

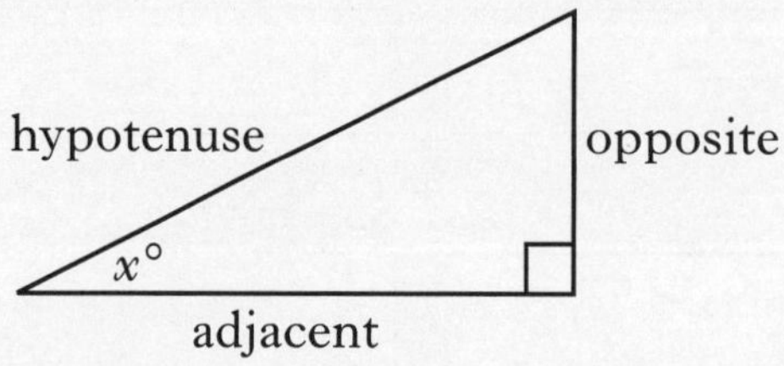

$$\tan x^\circ = \frac{\text{opposite}}{\text{adjacent}}$$

$$\sin x^\circ = \frac{\text{opposite}}{\text{hypotenuse}}$$

$$\cos x^\circ = \frac{\text{adjacent}}{\text{hypotenuse}}$$

Gradient:

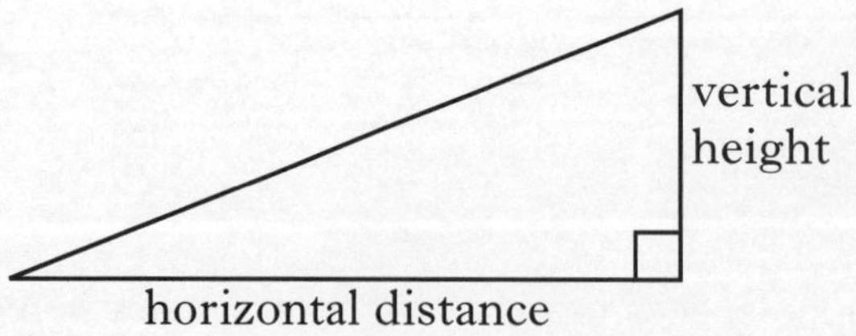

$$\text{Gradient} = \frac{\text{vertical height}}{\text{horizontal distance}}$$

DO NOT WRITE IN THIS MARGIN

Marks KU RE

1. A night train from London to Edinburgh leaves at 2321 and arrives at 0651.

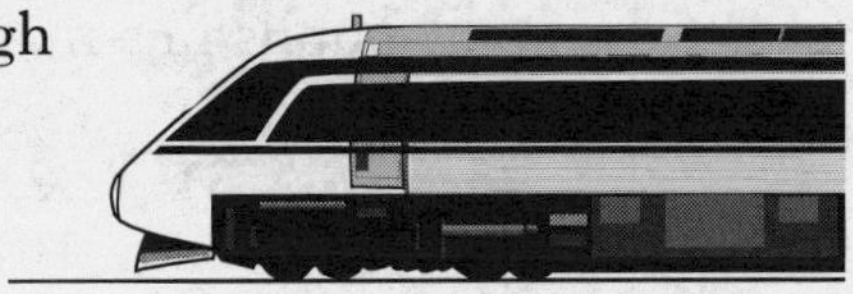

(*a*) How long does the train journey take? **2**

(*b*) The distance from London to Edinburgh is 644 kilometres.

Find the average speed of the train in kilometres per hour.

Give your answer correct to one decimal place. **3**

[Turn over

DO NOT WRITE IN THIS MARGIN

Marks | KU | RE

2. The marks of a group of pupils in a maths test are shown below.

43	17	25	25	29	31	32	11	26	20
25	42	32	33	25	28	41	35	32	26

(*a*) Illustrate this data in an ordered stem and leaf diagram. **3**

(*b*) What is the mode for the above data? **1**

DO NOT WRITE IN THIS MARGIN

Marks | KU | RE

3. Scott sees the following notice in the window of the Big Computer Shop.

The Big Computer Shop

Massive Sale

$33\frac{1}{3}$% discount

on all purchases

(*a*) A computer was £834.

How much would Scott pay for it in the sale? **2**

The same computer can be bought in Pete's PC Shop on hire purchase.

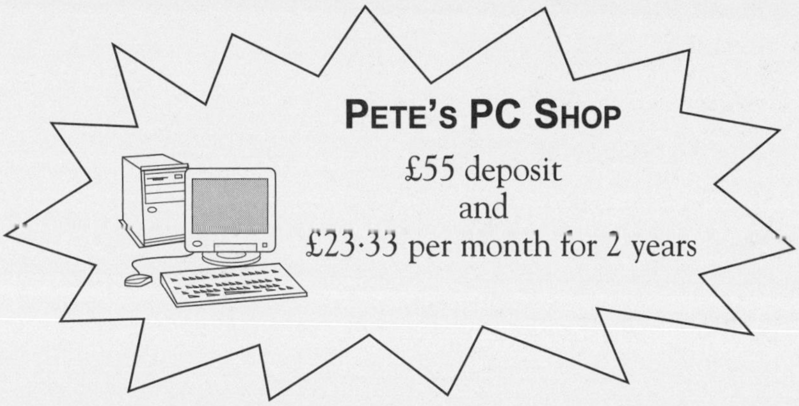

(*b*) Which shop sells the computer cheaper?

Show your working. **3**

DO NOT WRITE IN THIS MARGIN

Marks | KU | RE

4. The diagram below shows the shape of Sangita's garden.

Sangita plants a hedge along side AB.

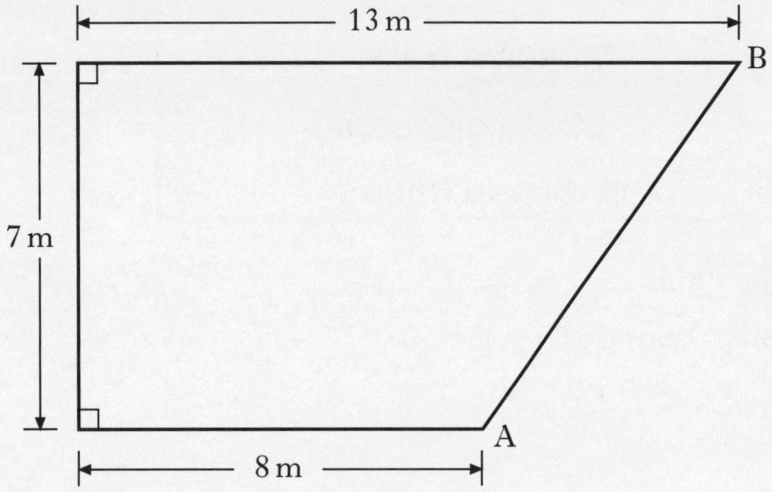

Calculate the length of the hedge.

4

DO NOT WRITE IN THIS MARGIN

Marks | KU | RE

5. (*a*) Remove the brackets and simplify

$$5 + 3(2x - 5).$$

2

(*b*) Solve the inequality

$$3x - 5 \geq 13.$$

2

[Turn over

DO NOT WRITE IN THIS MARGIN

Marks | KU | RE

6. The sponsors of the Champions league have given £900 000 to be shared among the four competing teams.

The league table is shown below.

The teams share the money in the ratio of the **points** they gain.

How much is **United's** share of the money?

	Played	Won	Lost	Drawn	Points
Inter	3	3	0	0	**9**
Athletic	3	2	1	0	**6**
United	3	1	2	0	**3**
Red Star	3	0	3	0	**0**

4

DO NOT WRITE IN THIS MARGIN

Marks | KU | RE

7. The diagram below shows Isla McGregor's electricity bill.

ScoPower Electricity				
Ms I McGregor 8 Birch Grove Pineford			Account No: 050621743X	
Statement Date: 20 April 2005		From: 21 Feb 2005	To: 18 Apr 2005	
Present reading	**Previous reading**	**Details of charges**		£
006890	006487	**Box A** [ ] units at 7·567p per unit		[·]
		Standing Charge		9·21
			Sub Total	[·]
			VAT @ 5%	[·]
			Total Charge	[·]

(*a*) Calculate the number of units used.

Write your answer in **Box A**. **1**

(*b*) Complete the electricity bill by filling in the shaded boxes. **3**

[Turn over

DO NOT WRITE IN THIS MARGIN

Marks | KU | RE

8. eSunTours is a holiday company.

Last year's percentage income from Skiing, Summer Tours, Winter Sun and Flights is shown in the pie chart below.

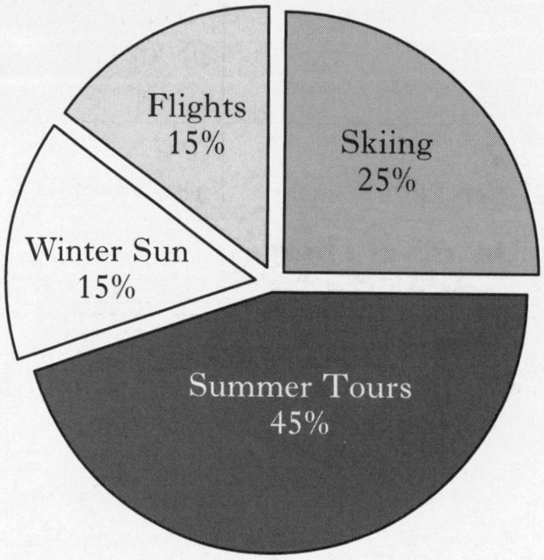

The income from Winter Sun holidays was £750 000 last year.

What was eSunTours' total income?

3

DO NOT WRITE IN THIS MARGIN

Marks | KU | RE

9. Serge drives from his home in Paris to Madrid, a journey of 1280 kilometres.

His car has a 60 litre petrol tank and travels 13 kilometres per litre.

Serge starts his journey with a full tank of petrol.

What is the least number of times he has to stop to refuel?

Give a reason for your answer.

3

[Turn over

DO NOT WRITE IN THIS MARGIN

Marks | KU | RE

10. (*a*) The edge of a stock cube measures 1·5 centimetres.

Calculate the volume of the stock cube.

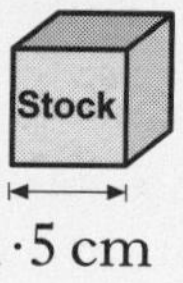

1

(*b*) A number of the above stock cubes are packed into a cuboid box.

The box is 6 centimetres long, 3 centimetres broad and 9 centimetres high.

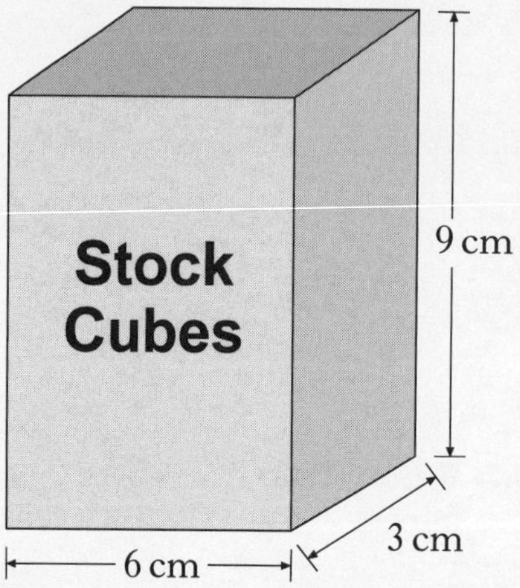

How many stock cubes are needed to fill the box?

3

DO NOT WRITE IN THIS MARGIN

Marks KU RE

11.

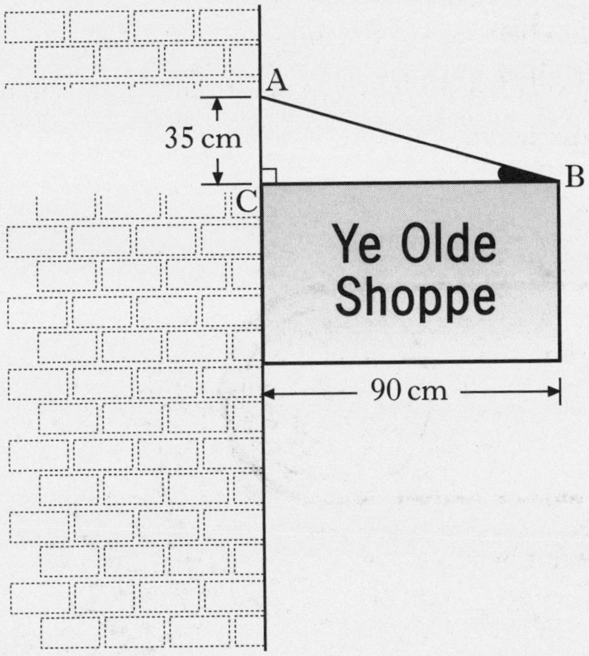

A rectangular shop sign is supported by a metal bar AB.

The length of the shop sign is 90 centimetres and the bar AB is attached to the wall 35 centimetres above the sign.

Calculate the size of the shaded angle ABC.

Do not use a scale drawing. 3

[Turn over for Question 12 on *Page fourteen*

DO NOT WRITE IN THIS MARGIN

Marks | KU | RE

12. The diagram below shows the fan belt from a machine.

The fan belt passes around 2 wheels whose centres are 30 centimetres apart.

Each wheel is 8 centimetres in diameter.

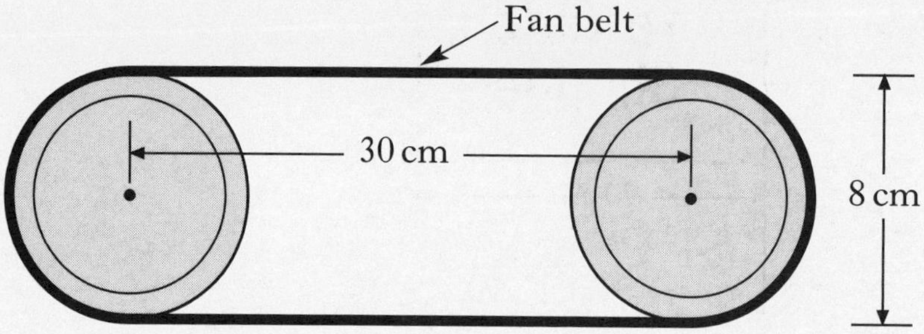

Calculate the total length of the fan belt.

4

[*END OF QUESTION PAPER*]

ADDITIONAL SPACE FOR ANSWERS

ADDITIONAL SPACE FOR ANSWERS

[BLANK PAGE]

FOR OFFICIAL USE

G

	KU	RE
Total marks		

2500/403

NATIONAL QUALIFICATIONS 2006

FRIDAY, 5 MAY
10.40 AM – 11.15 AM

MATHEMATICS
STANDARD GRADE
General Level
Paper 1
Non-calculator

Fill in these boxes and read what is printed below.

Full name of centre

Town

Forename(s)

Surname

Date of birth
Day Month Year

Scottish candidate number

Number of seat

1 **You may not use a calculator.**

2 Answer as many questions as you can.

3 Write your working and answers in the spaces provided. Additional space is provided at the end of this question-answer book for use if required. If you use this space, write clearly the number of the question involved.

4 Full credit will be given only where the solution contains appropriate working.

5 Before leaving the examination room you must give this book to the invigilator. If you do not you may lose all the marks for this paper.

SCOTTISH QUALIFICATIONS AUTHORITY

LI 2500/403 6/64470

FORMULAE LIST

Circumference of a circle:	$C = \pi d$
Area of a circle:	$A = \pi r^2$
Curved surface area of a cylinder:	$A = 2\pi rh$
Volume of a cylinder:	$V = \pi r^2 h$
Volume of a triangular prism:	$V = Ah$

Theorem of Pythagoras:

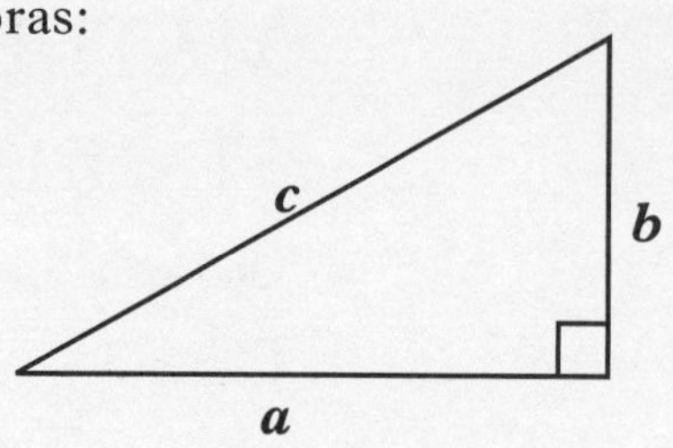

$$a^2 + b^2 = c^2$$

Trigonometric ratios in a right angled triangle:

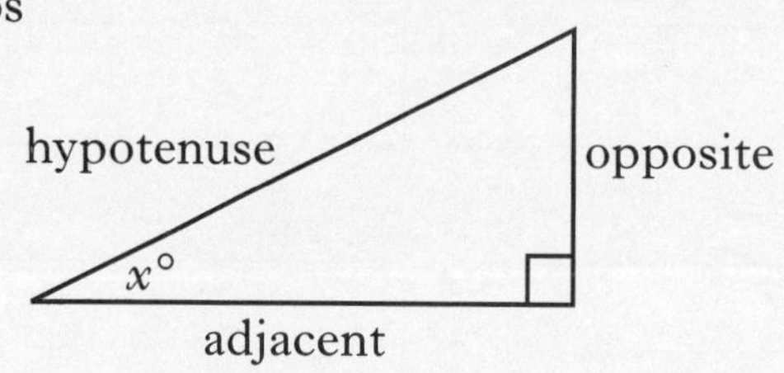

$$\tan x° = \frac{\textbf{opposite}}{\textbf{adjacent}}$$

$$\sin x° = \frac{\textbf{opposite}}{\textbf{hypotenuse}}$$

$$\cos x° = \frac{\textbf{adjacent}}{\textbf{hypotenuse}}$$

Gradient:

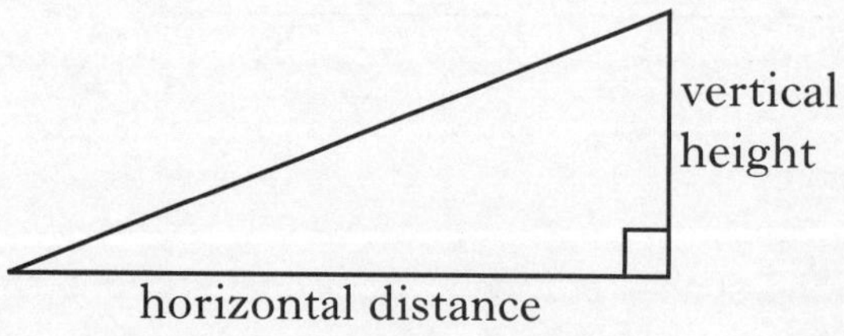

$$\textbf{Gradient} = \frac{\textbf{vertical height}}{\textbf{horizontal distance}}$$

DO NOT WRITE IN THIS MARGIN

Marks KU RE

1. Carry out the following calculations.

(*a*) $2{\cdot}73 + 7{\cdot}6 - 8{\cdot}4$ **1**

(*b*) 13×7000 **1**

(*c*) $56{\cdot}5 \div 500$ **1**

(*d*) 30% of 92 litres **2**

[Turn over

Marks | KU | RE

2.

Paulo's Pizzas

Student Discount

$\frac{1}{3}$ off the price of each pizza

Emily is a student and she buys a pizza from Paulo's Pizzas.

She chooses a pizza which is normally £8·49.

How much will Emily pay for the pizza? **3**

3. A new movie costs $320 million to make.

Write this amount in scientific notation.

2

DO NOT WRITE IN THIS MARGIN

Marks KU RE

4. Jenni is making a wallpaper border.

She is using stars and dots to make the border.

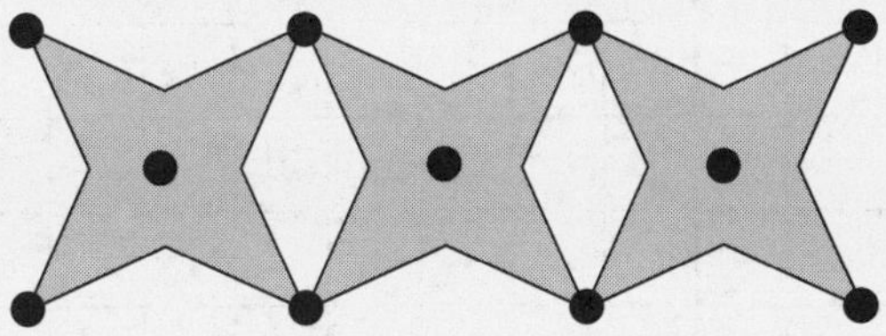

(*a*) Complete the table below.

Number of stars (s)	1	2	3	4	5
Number of dots (d)			11		

2

(*b*) Write down a formula for calculating the number of dots (d), when you know the number of stars (s).

2

(*c*) Each star is 10 centimetres long.

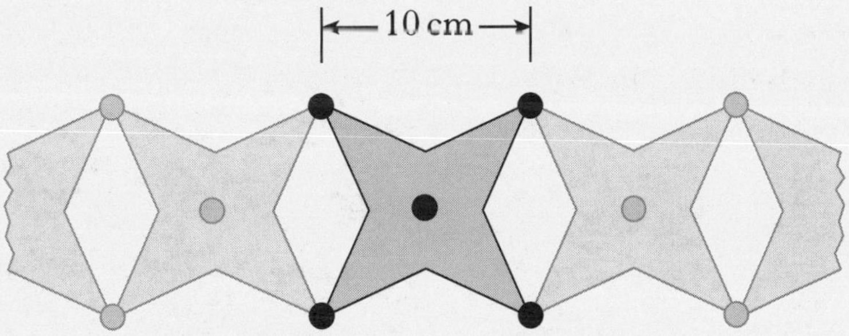

The wallpaper border Jenni makes is 300 centimetres long.

(i) How many stars does Jenni need?

1

(ii) How many dots does she need?

2

DO NOT WRITE IN THIS MARGIN

Marks	KU	RE

5. The line AB is drawn on the grid below.

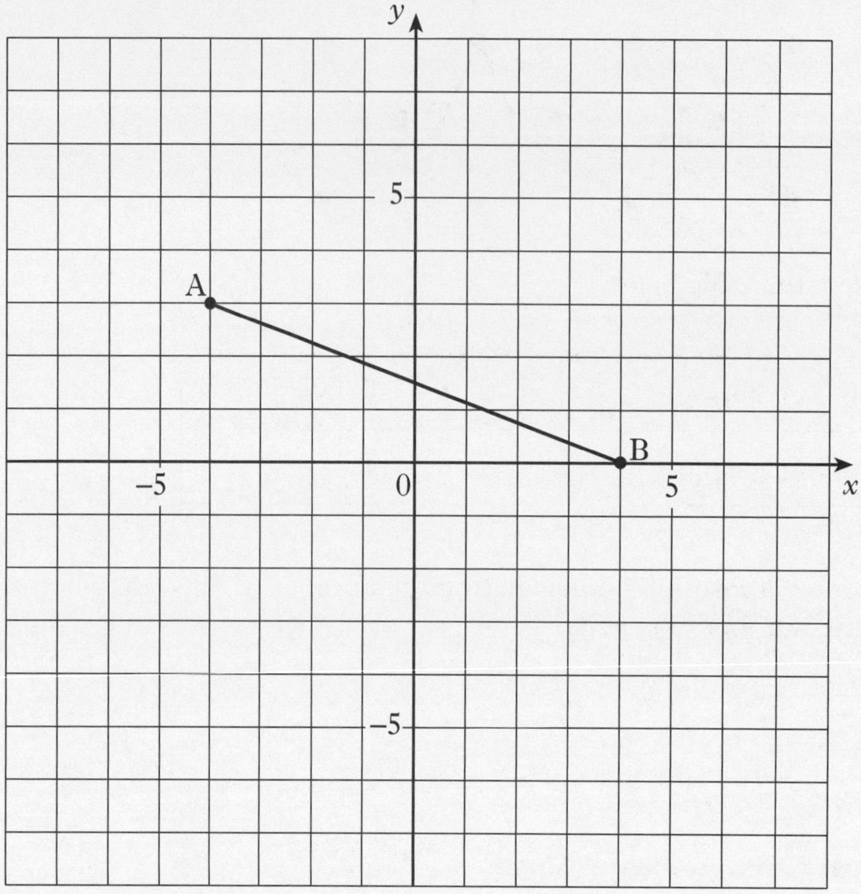

Calculate the gradient of the line AB. **2**

DO NOT WRITE IN THIS MARGIN

Marks | KU | RE

6. A box contains 10 coloured balls.

There are 4 yellow balls, 3 blue balls, 2 green balls and 1 red ball.

(*a*) David takes a ball from the box.

What is the probability that the ball is blue? **1**

(*b*) The ball is put back in the box.

2 yellow balls and the red ball are then removed.

What is the probability that the next ball David takes from the box is green? **2**

[Turn over

DO NOT WRITE IN THIS MARGIN

Marks	KU	RE

7. The temperature in a supermarket freezer during a 12-hour period is shown in the graph below.

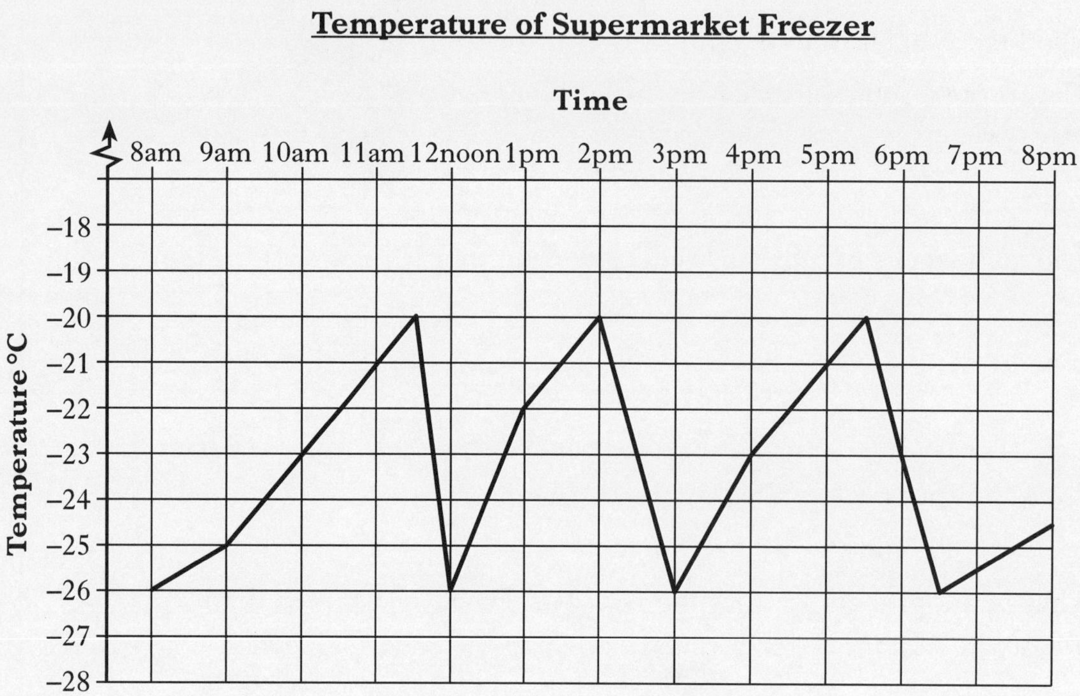

(*a*) From 8am, how long did it take for the temperature to rise to −20 °C? **1**

(*b*) For how long, in **total**, was the temperature rising during the 12-hour period? **3**

DO NOT WRITE IN THIS MARGIN

Marks | KU | RE

8. Rachel asks 19 friends how many text messages they sent last week.

Their answers are shown below.

34	25	46	62	28
38	42	23	25	15
32	52	35	44	30
10	33	41	55	

(*a*) Display Rachel's friends' answers in an ordered stem and leaf diagram. **3**

(*b*) What is the median number of text messages? **1**

[Turn over for Question 9 on *Page ten*

DO NOT WRITE IN THIS MARGIN

Marks | KU | RE

9.

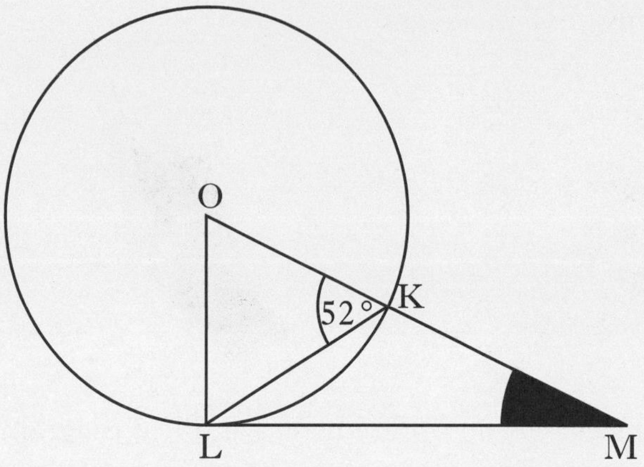

In the diagram above with circle centre O:

- LM is a tangent to the circle at L
- OM intersects the circle at K
- Angle OKL = 52°.

Calculate the size of the shaded angle OML.

3

[*END OF QUESTION PAPER*]

ADDITIONAL SPACE FOR ANSWERS

ADDITIONAL SPACE FOR ANSWERS

FOR OFFICIAL USE

G

	KU	RE
Total marks		

2500/404

NATIONAL QUALIFICATIONS 2006

FRIDAY, 5 MAY
11.35 AM – 12.30 PM

MATHEMATICS
STANDARD GRADE
General Level
Paper 2

Fill in these boxes and read what is printed below.

Full name of centre

Town

Forename(s)

Surname

Date of birth
Day Month Year

Scottish candidate number

Number of seat

1 **You may use a calculator.**

2 Answer as many questions as you can.

3 Write your working and answers in the spaces provided. Additional space is provided at the end of this question-answer book for use if required. If you use this space, write clearly the number of the question involved.

4 Full credit will be given only where the solution contains appropriate working.

5 Before leaving the examination room you must give this book to the invigilator. If you do not you may lose all the marks for this paper.

SCOTTISH QUALIFICATIONS AUTHORITY

FORMULAE LIST

Circumference of a circle: $C = \pi d$

Area of a circle: $A = \pi r^2$

Curved surface area of a cylinder: $A = 2\pi rh$

Volume of a cylinder: $V = \pi r^2 h$

Volume of a triangular prism: $V = Ah$

Theorem of Pythagoras:

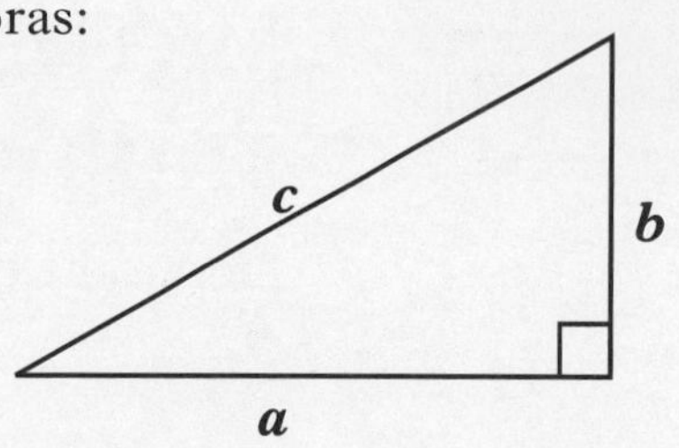

$a^2 + b^2 = c^2$

Trigonometric ratios in a right angled triangle:

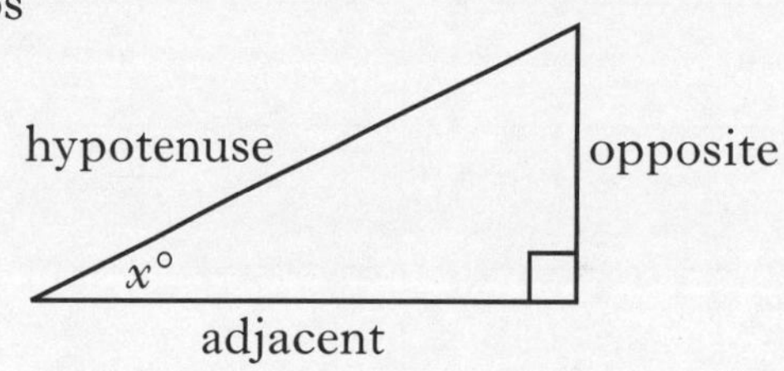

$\tan x° = \frac{\text{opposite}}{\text{adjacent}}$

$\sin x° = \frac{\text{opposite}}{\text{hypotenuse}}$

$\cos x° = \frac{\text{adjacent}}{\text{hypotenuse}}$

Gradient:

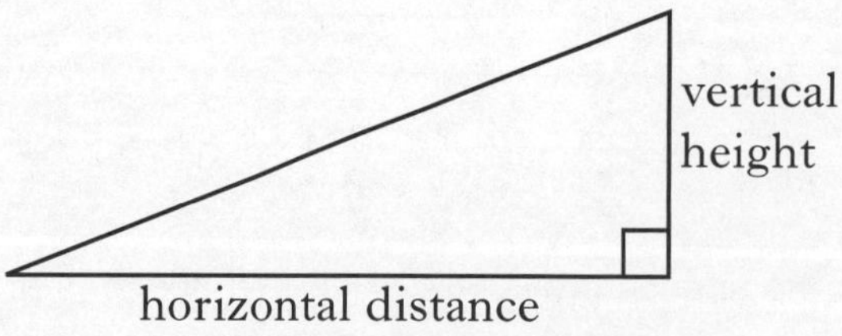

$\text{Gradient} = \frac{\text{vertical height}}{\text{horizontal distance}}$

DO NOT WRITE IN THIS MARGIN

Marks | KU | RE

1. The Sharkey family is going on holiday to France.

They will stay at the "Prenez Les Bains" campsite.

Prenez Les Bains	Tent holiday		Mobile Home holiday	
Start Date	Cost for 7 nights	Cost per extra night	Cost for 7 nights	Cost per extra night
26 June – 2 July	495	39	585	58
3 July – 9 July	535	41	615	65
10 July – 30 July	645	46	825	72
31 July – 13 Aug	699	47	880	75
14 Aug – 28 Aug	670	39	845	73

The family chooses a mobile home holiday.

Their holiday will start on 15 July and the family will stay for 12 nights.

Use the table above to calculate the cost of the holiday. **3**

[Turn over

DO NOT WRITE IN THIS MARGIN

Marks | KU | RE

2. Carly bought a new printer for her computer.

The time taken to print a document is proportional to the number of pages printed.

It takes 7 minutes to print a document with 63 pages.

How many pages can be printed in half an hour?

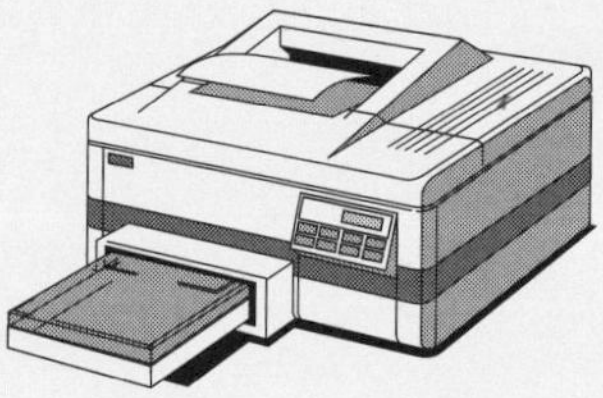

3

DO NOT WRITE IN THIS MARGIN

Marks KU RE

3. At a school fun day, prizes can be won by throwing darts at a target.

Each person throws **six** darts.

Points are awarded as follows.

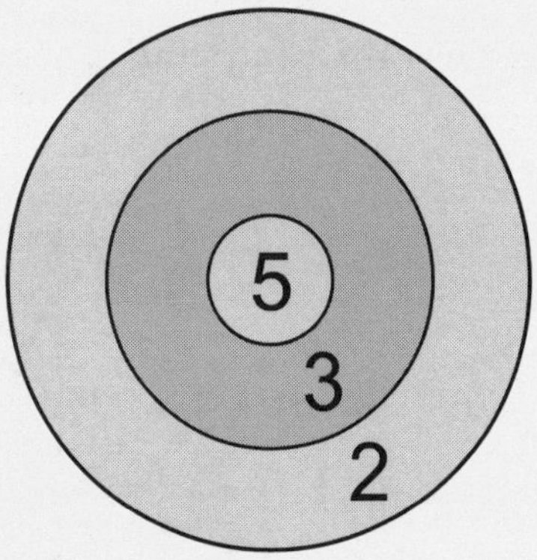

	POINTS
Centre	5
Middle Ring	3
Outer Ring	2
Miss	0

Prizes are won for **25 points or more**.

Complete the table below to show all the different ways to win a prize.

Number of darts scoring 5 points	Number of darts scoring 3 points	Number of darts scoring 2 points	Number of darts scoring 0 points	Total Points
4	2	0	0	26

4

[Turn over

DO NOT WRITE IN THIS MARGIN

Marks | KU | RE

4. The entrance to a building is by a ramp as shown in the diagram below.

The length of the ramp is 180 centimetres.

The angle between the ramp and the ground is 12°.

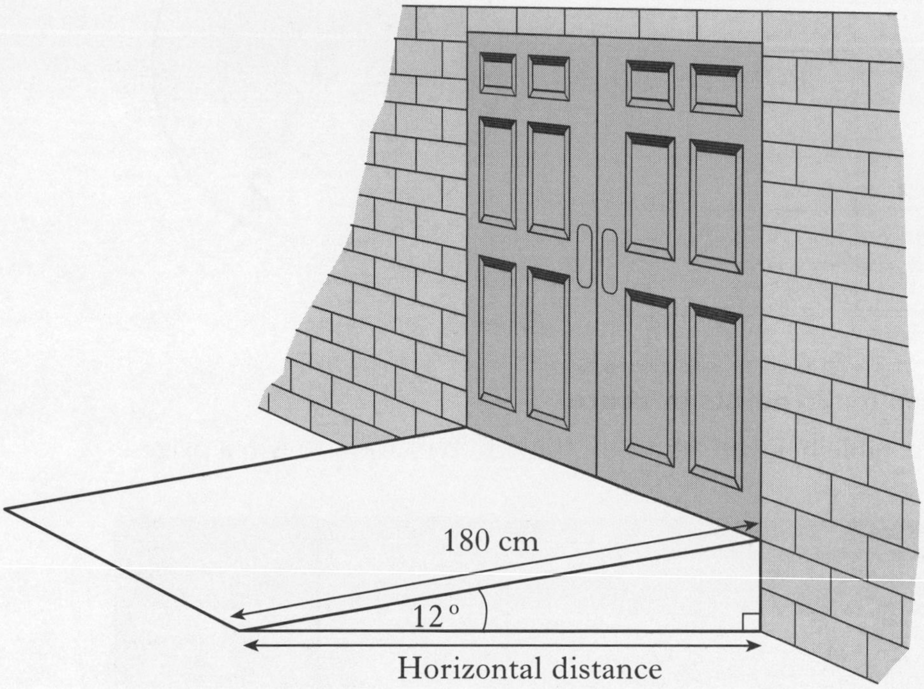

Calculate the horizontal distance.

Round your answer to one decimal place.

Do not use a scale drawing.

4

DO NOT WRITE IN THIS MARGIN

Marks | KU | RE

5. Ann works in a hotel.

She is paid £5·60 per hour on weekdays and double time at weekends.

Last month her gross pay was £436·80.

Ann worked a total of 54 hours on weekdays.

How many hours did she work at double time?

4

[Turn over

DO NOT WRITE IN THIS MARGIN

Marks | KU | RE

6. (*a*) Factorise

$$6a + 15b.$$

2

(*b*) Solve algebraically

$$4x - 3 = x + 21.$$

3

DO NOT WRITE IN THIS MARGIN

Marks | KU | RE

7. Amy and Brian travel from Dundee to Stonehaven.

The distance between Dundee and Stonehaven is 80 kilometres.

Amy takes 1 hour 30 minutes to travel by car.

Brian takes the train which travels at an average speed of 60 kilometres per hour.

What is the difference between their journey times?

4

[Turn over

DO NOT WRITE IN THIS MARGIN

Marks | KU | RE

8. ABCD is a rhombus.

AE = 4·3 metres and BE = 2·9 metres.

Calculate the perimeter of the rhombus.

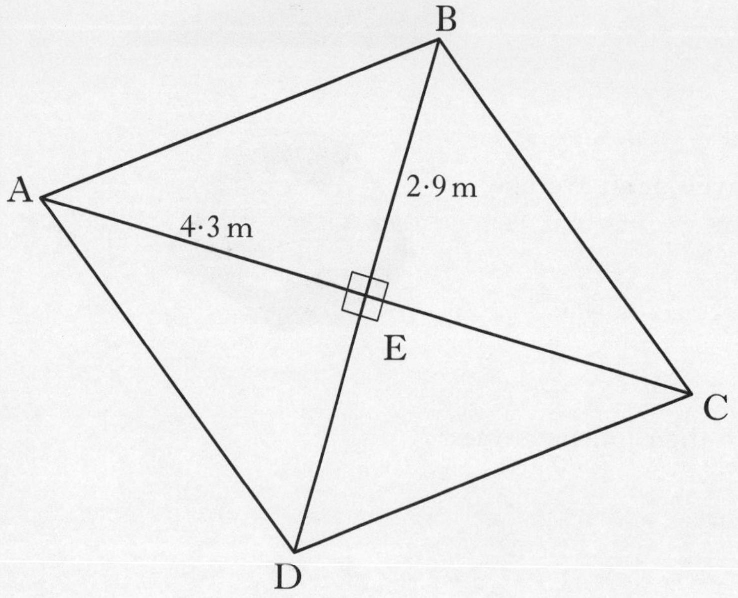

Do not use a scale drawing.

4

DO NOT WRITE IN THIS MARGIN

Marks	KU	RE

9. The top of Calum's desk is in the shape of a quarter-circle as shown.

The measurement shown is in metres.

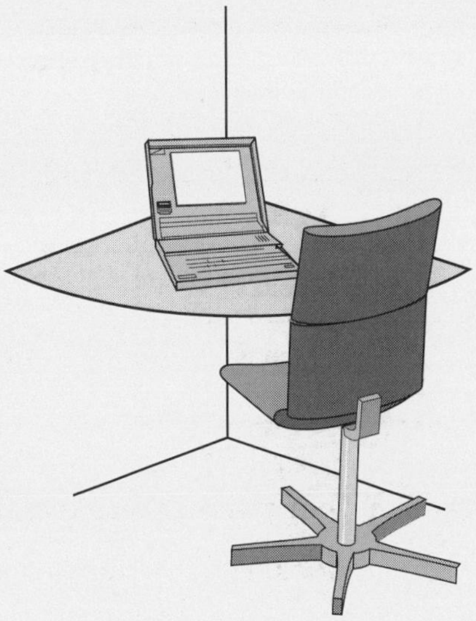

(*a*) Calculate the area of the top of the desk. **2**

(*b*) Calum wants to paint the top of his desk.

The tin of paint he buys has a coverage of $1\,m^2$.

Using this tin of paint, how many times could he paint the top of his desk? **2**

DO NOT WRITE IN THIS MARGIN

Marks | KU | RE

10. Maria is two years old.

Each week she goes to the nursery for 3 full days and 2 half days.

(*a*)

Playwell Nursery

	Prices	
Age	**Full day**	**Half day**
0–2 years	£28	£15
3–5 years	£23·50	£12·50

Maria's mother pays for her to attend Playwell Nursery.

How much does Maria's mother pay each week? 2

On Monday, Tuesday and Wednesday Maria goes to nursery from 9 am to 3 pm.

On Thursday and Friday she goes from 9 am to 12 noon.

(*b*) The nursery introduces a new hourly rate.

New Rate £5 per hour

Will Maria's mother save money when the nursery changes to the hourly rate?

Give a reason for your answer. 3

DO NOT WRITE IN THIS MARGIN

Marks | KU | RE

11. The diagram below shows the positions of Lossiemouth and Leuchars.

A ship in the North Sea is on a bearing of 110° from Lossiemouth and 075° from Leuchars.

Show the position of the ship on the diagram below.

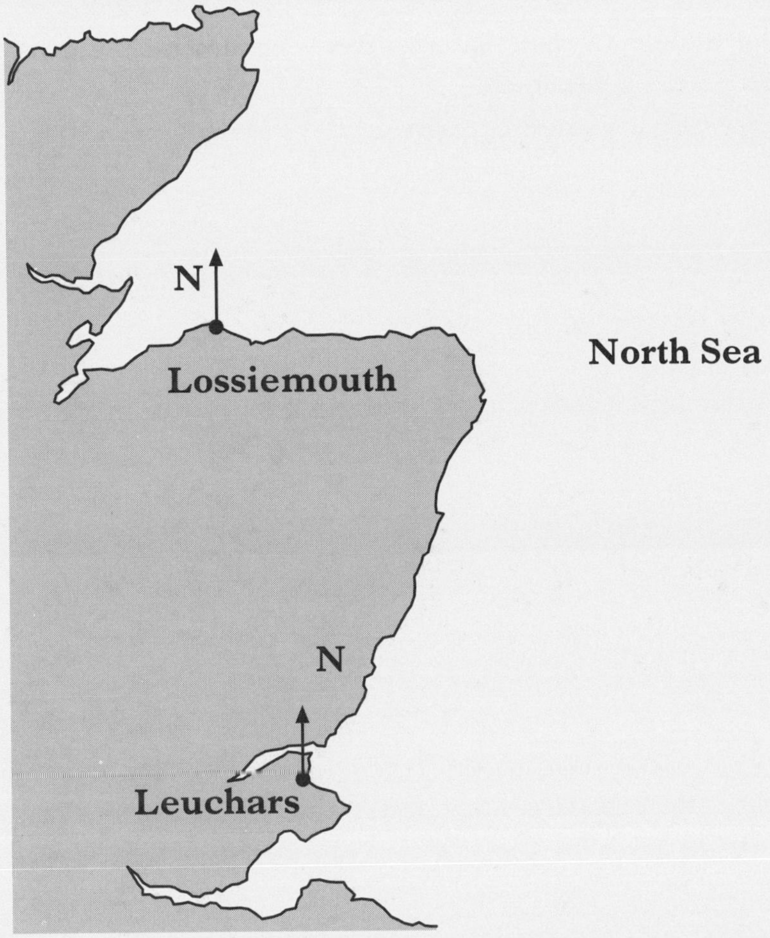

3

[Turn over for Question 12 on *Page fourteen*

DO NOT WRITE IN THIS MARGIN

Marks | KU | RE

12. Gordon is insuring his car with Carins Insurance.

The basic annual premium is £765.

As Gordon is a new customer his premium is calculated by taking $\frac{1}{5}$ off the basic annual premium.

However, because he wants to pay in monthly instalments, Carins Insurance add an extra 8% to his premium.

How much in total will Gordon pay per month? **4**

[*END OF QUESTION PAPER*]

ADDITIONAL SPACE FOR ANSWERS

ADDITIONAL SPACE FOR ANSWERS

[BLANK PAGE]

FOR OFFICIAL USE

G

	KU	RE
Total marks		

2500/403

NATIONAL QUALIFICATIONS 2007

THURSDAY, 3 MAY
10.40 AM – 11.15 AM

MATHEMATICS STANDARD GRADE

General Level
Paper 1
Non-calculator

Fill in these boxes and read what is printed below.

Full name of centre

Town

Forename(s)

Surname

Date of birth
Day Month Year

Scottish candidate number

Number of seat

1 **You may not use a calculator.**

2 Answer as many questions as you can.

3 Write your working and answers in the spaces provided. Additional space is provided at the end of this question-answer book for use if required. If you use this space, write clearly the number of the question involved.

4 Full credit will be given only where the solution contains appropriate working.

5 Before leaving the examination room you must give this book to the invigilator. If you do not you may lose all the marks for this paper.

FORMULAE LIST

Circumference of a circle: $C = \pi d$

Area of a circle: $A = \pi r^2$

Curved surface area of a cylinder: $A = 2\pi rh$

Volume of a cylinder: $V = \pi r^2 h$

Volume of a triangular prism: $V = Ah$

Theorem of Pythagoras:

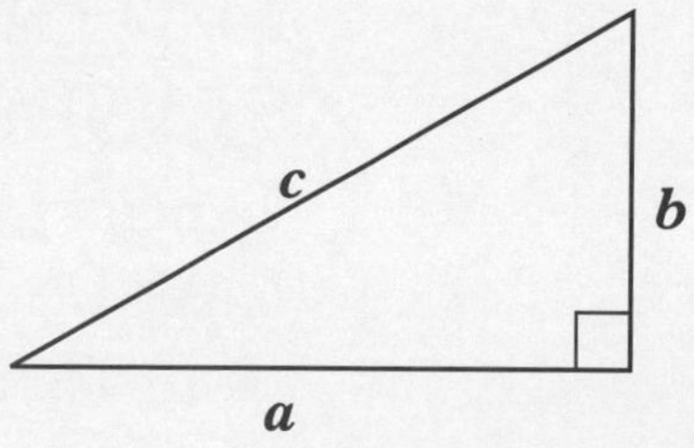

$$a^2 + b^2 = c^2$$

Trigonometric ratios in a right angled triangle:

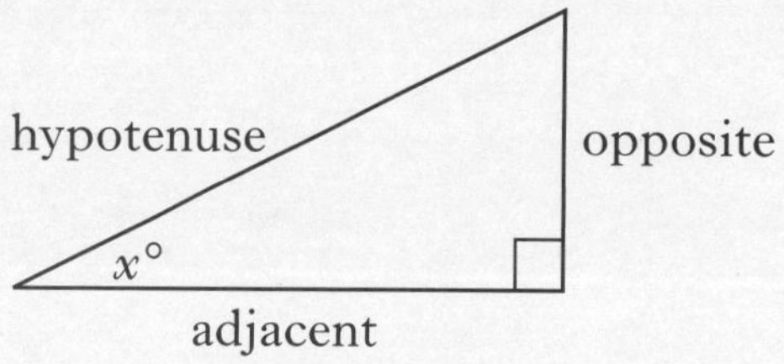

$$\tan x^\circ = \frac{\text{opposite}}{\text{adjacent}}$$

$$\sin x^\circ = \frac{\text{opposite}}{\text{hypotenuse}}$$

$$\cos x^\circ = \frac{\text{adjacent}}{\text{hypotenuse}}$$

Gradient:

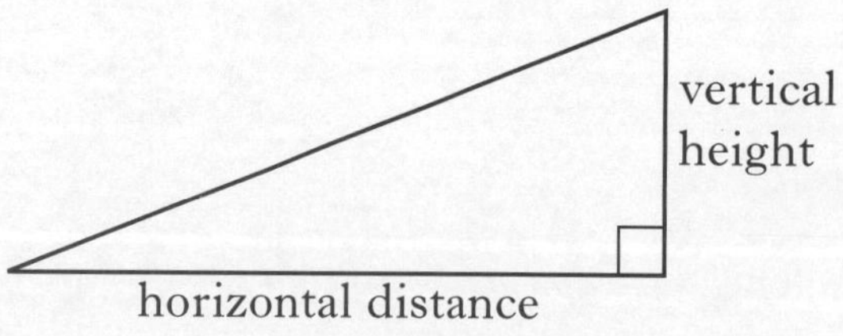

$$\text{Gradient} = \frac{\text{vertical height}}{\text{horizontal distance}}$$

DO NOT WRITE IN THIS MARGIN

Marks	KU	RE

1. Carry out the following calculations.

(*a*) $4{\cdot}27 - 1{\cdot}832$

4·270
−1·832
2·438

1

(*b*) $6{\cdot}53 \times 40$

6.53
× 40
141·20

1

(*c*) $372 \div 8$

046·5
8 ⟌ 372·0

46·5

1

(*d*) $5 \times 4\frac{1}{3}$

$\frac{5}{1} \times \frac{13}{3}$

$= \frac{65}{3}$

2

2. A particle is radioactive for $2{\cdot}3 \times 10^{-4}$ seconds.

Write this number in full.

0·00023

2

DO NOT WRITE IN THIS MARGIN

Marks | KU | RE

3. Zoe is a member of a gym.

The gym offers the following exercise sessions.

Exercise	Session Time
Weights	15 minutes
Dance	40 minutes
Running	20 minutes
Cycling	30 minutes
Swimming	45 minutes

Zoe is advised to choose **three** different exercises.

She wants to exercise for a **minimum of 90 minutes**.

One possible combination of three different exercises is shown in the table below.

Complete the table to show all the possible combinations of three different exercises Zoe can choose.

Weights	Dance	Running	Cycling	Swimming	Total Time (minutes)
		✓	✓	✓	95 minutes
✓	✓			✓	100 minutes
	✓	✓	✓		90 minutes
✓			✓	✓	90 mins
	✓	✓		✓	105 minutes

3

DO NOT WRITE IN THIS MARGIN

Marks	KU	RE

4. Complete this shape so that it has quarter-turn symmetry about O.

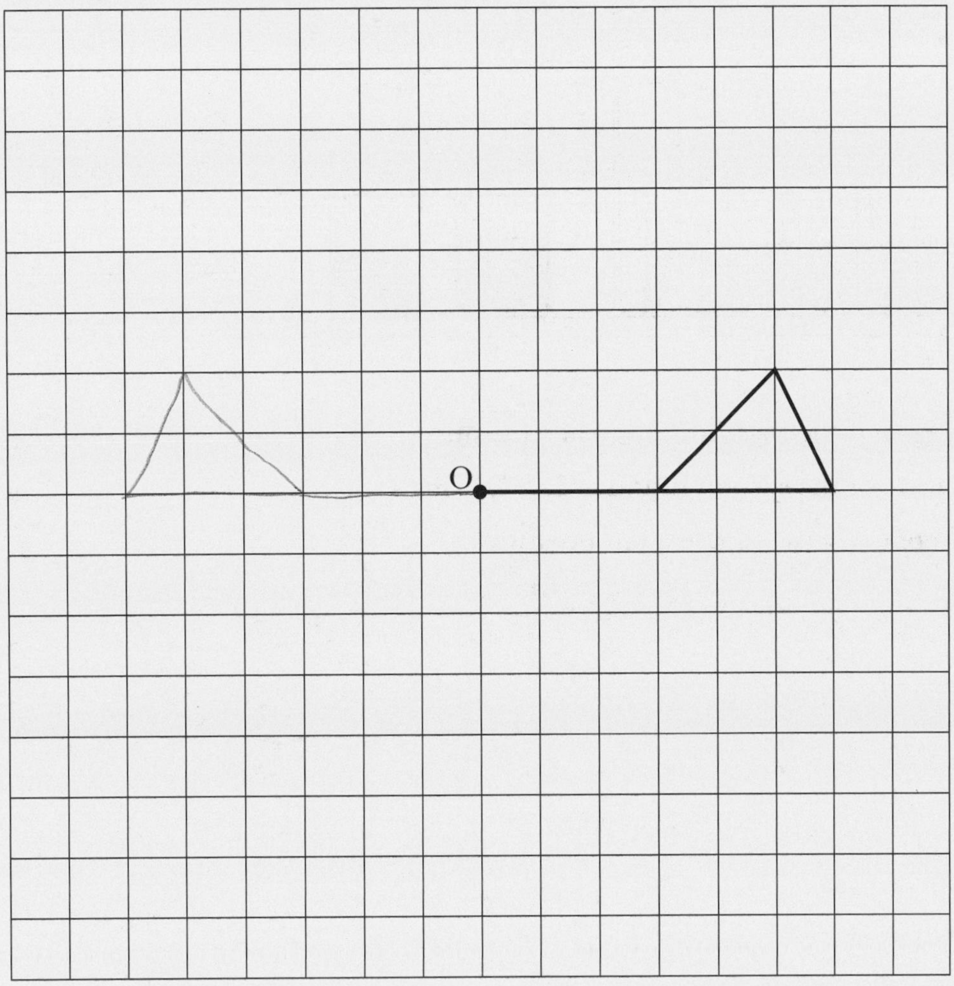

3

[Turn over

DO NOT WRITE IN THIS MARGIN

Marks | KU | RE

5. In an experiment Rashid measures the temperature of two liquids.

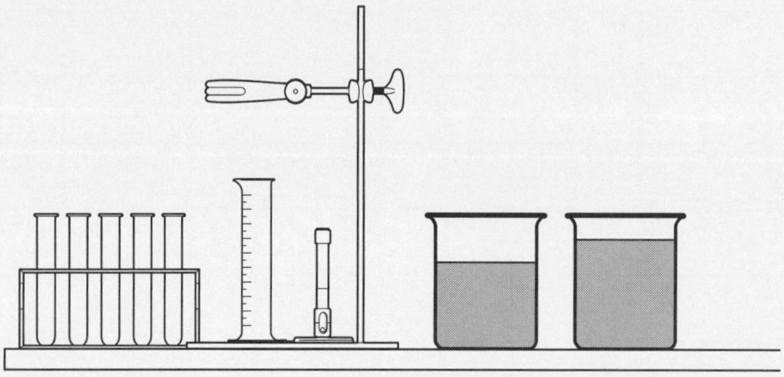

The temperature of the first liquid is –11 ° Celsius.

The temperature of the second liquid is 23 ° Celsius.

Find the difference between these temperatures. **2**

23
+11
34

34° difference

DO NOT WRITE IN THIS MARGIN

Marks KU RE

6. A children's play area is to be fenced.

The fence is made in sections using lengths of wood, as shown below.

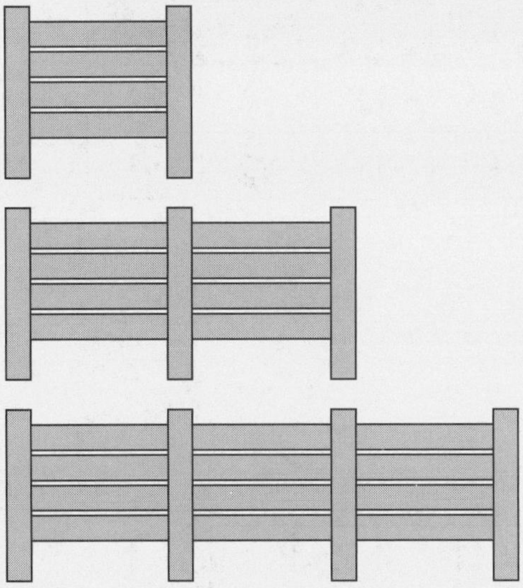

1 section

2 sections

3 sections

(*a*) Complete the table below.

Number of sections (s)	1	2	3	4	5	10	12
Number of lengths of wood (w)	6	11	16	21	26	51	61

2

(*b*) Write down a formula for calculating the number of lengths of wood (w), when you know the number of sections (s).

$S = 5w + 1$

2

(*c*) A fence has been made from 81 lengths of wood.

How many sections are in this fence?

You must show your working.

$80 - 1 = 80$

$5 \overline{)80} = 16$

16 sections

2

DO NOT WRITE IN THIS MARGIN

Marks | KU | RE

7. The table below shows the marks scored by pupils in French and Italian exams.

Pupil	A	B	C	D	E	F	G	H
French Mark	15	23	50	38	40	42	70	82
Italian Mark	28	31	62	54	45	55	85	95

(*a*) Using these marks, draw a scattergraph. **2**

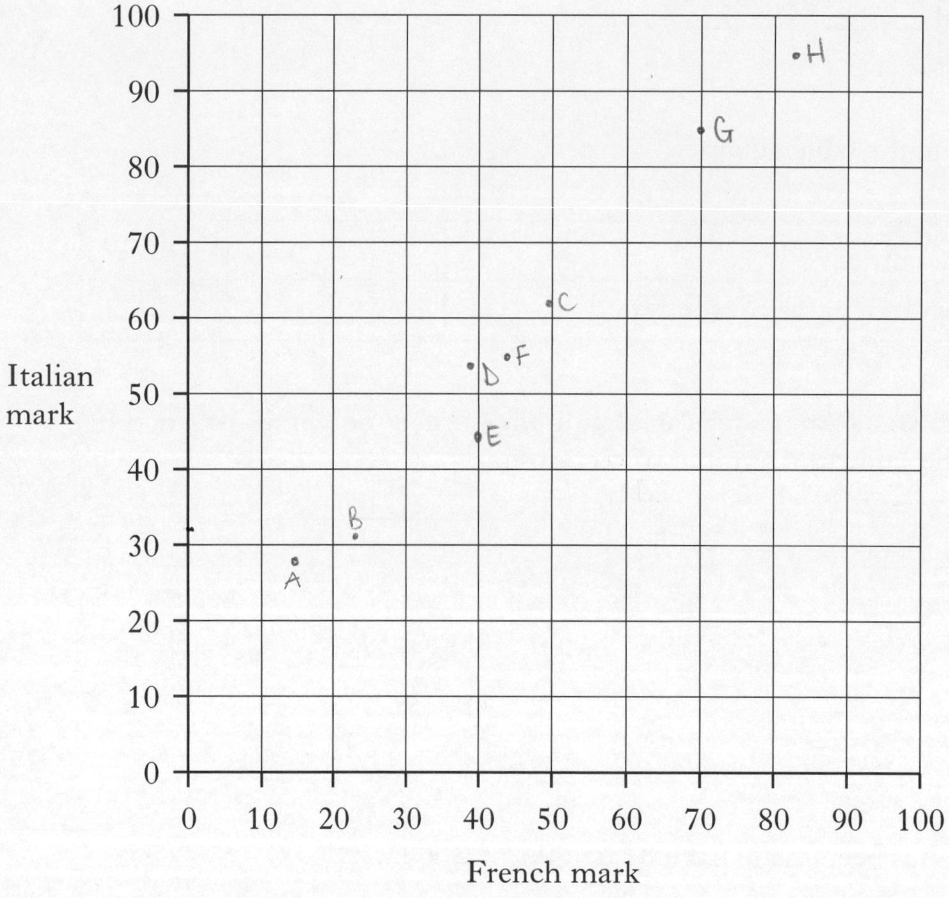

(*b*) Draw a best-fitting line on the graph. **1**

DO NOT WRITE IN THIS MARGIN

Marks | KU | RE

7. (continued)

(*c*) A pupil who scored 65 in his French exam was absent from the Italian exam.

Use your best-fitting line to estimate this pupil's Italian mark. **1**

8. Pamela sees a bracelet costing £65 in a jeweller's window.

The jeweller offers Pamela a 5% discount.

Pamela decides to buy the bracelet.

How much does she pay?

5% of £65

5% = (65 ÷ 10) ÷ 2 = 3·25

65·00
3·25
61·75

3

DO NOT WRITE IN THIS MARGIN

Marks | KU | RE

9. Craig works in the school office.

Shown below is his order for 25 boxes of folders.

Office Supplies	
Blue Folders	7 boxes
Green Folders	11 boxes
Pink Folders	3 boxes
Yellow Folders	4 boxes
Total	**25 boxes**

His order has arrived in identical boxes but they are not labelled.

(*a*) What is the probability that the first box Craig opens contains pink folders?

$\frac{3}{25}$ chances

1

(*b*) The first box Craig opens contains green folders.

What is the probability that the next box he opens contains blue folders?

$25 - 11 = 14$ → $\frac{7}{14}$ $\frac{1}{2}$ chances

2

DO NOT WRITE IN THIS MARGIN

Marks	KU	RE

10. There are 720 pupils in Laggan High School.

The ratio of boys to girls in the school is 5 : 4.

How many girls are in the school?

080
9)720

80
×4
320

320 girls

3

[*END OF QUESTION PAPER*]

ADDITIONAL SPACE FOR ANSWERS

FOR OFFICIAL USE

G

	KU	RE
Total marks		

2500/404

NATIONAL QUALIFICATIONS 2007

THURSDAY, 3 MAY
11.35 AM – 12.30 PM

MATHEMATICS
STANDARD GRADE
General Level
Paper 2

Fill in these boxes and read what is printed below.

Full name of centre

Town

Forename(s)

Surname

Date of birth
Day Month Year

Scottish candidate number

Number of seat

1 **You may use a calculator.**

2 Answer as many questions as you can.

3 Write your working and answers in the spaces provided. Additional space is provided at the end of this question-answer book for use if required. If you use this space, write clearly the number of the question involved.

4 Full credit will be given only where the solution contains appropriate working.

5 Before leaving the examination room you must give this book to the invigilator. If you do not you may lose all the marks for this paper.

SCOTTISH QUALIFICATIONS AUTHORITY

LI 2500/404 6/68370

FORMULAE LIST

Circumference of a circle:	$C = \pi d$
Area of a circle:	$A = \pi r^2$
Curved surface area of a cylinder:	$A = 2\pi rh$
Volume of a cylinder:	$V = \pi r^2 h$
Volume of a triangular prism:	$V = Ah$

Theorem of Pythagoras:

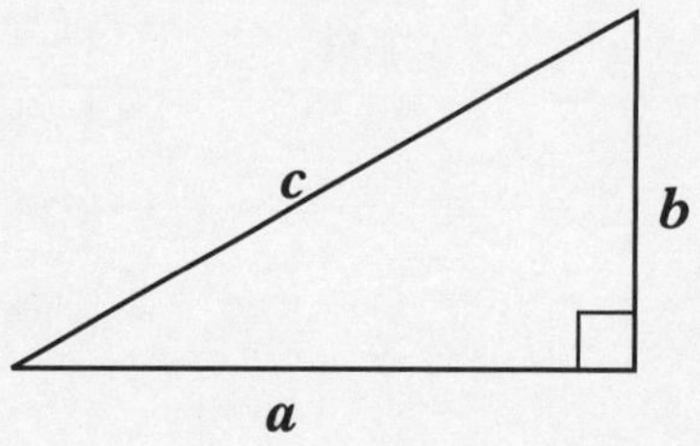

$$a^2 + b^2 = c^2$$

Trigonometric ratios in a right angled triangle:

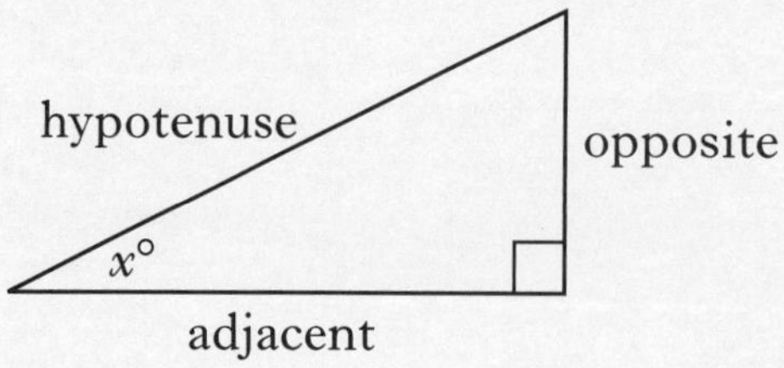

$$\tan x^\circ = \frac{\text{opposite}}{\text{adjacent}}$$

$$\sin x^\circ = \frac{\text{opposite}}{\text{hypotenuse}}$$

$$\cos x^\circ = \frac{\text{adjacent}}{\text{hypotenuse}}$$

Gradient:

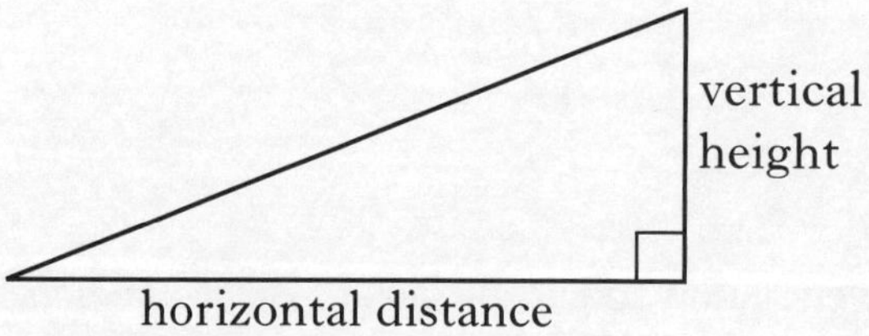

$$\text{Gradient} = \frac{\text{vertical height}}{\text{horizontal distance}}$$

DO NOT WRITE IN THIS MARGIN

Marks | KU | RE

1. A Sprinter train travels at an average speed of 144 kilometres per hour.

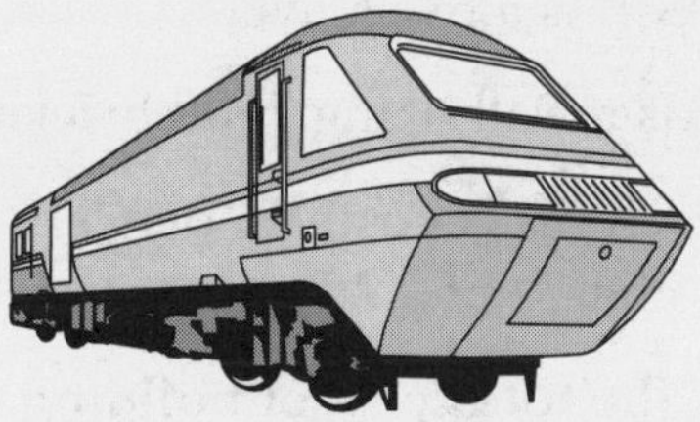

The train takes 1 hour 15 minutes to travel between Dingwall and Aberdeen.

Calculate the distance between Dingwall and Aberdeen.

2

[Turn over

DO NOT WRITE IN THIS MARGIN

Marks | KU | RE

2. Mr McGill is a bricklayer.

He builds a wall using 7500 bricks:

- each brick costs 23 pence
- a charge of £200 is made for every 500 bricks he lays.

What is the **total** cost of building the wall?

3

DO NOT WRITE IN THIS MARGIN

Marks | KU | RE

3.

BELMONT VETS
CHECK-UP FEES

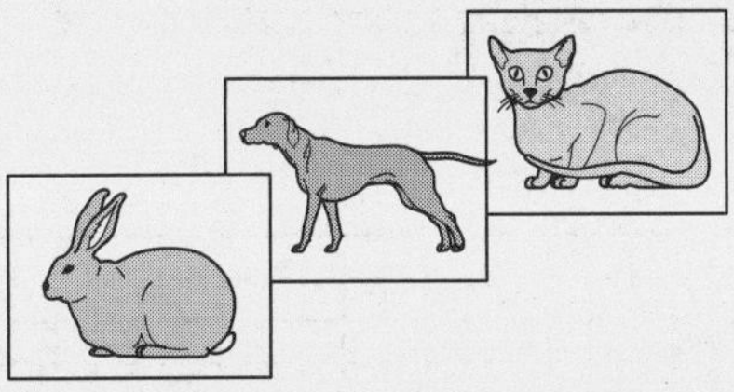

Dog	**£17·50**
Cat	**£11·75**
Rabbit	**£7·95**

The Wilson family owns two dogs and a cat.

Last year each dog had two check-ups at Belmont Vets.

The family cat also had check-ups last year.

The Wilson's total check-up fees for the two dogs and the cat were £105·25.

How often did the cat have a check-up?

4

[Turn over

DO NOT WRITE IN THIS MARGIN

Marks | KU | RE

4. A rectangular metal grill for a window is shown below.

Two diagonal metal bars strengthen the grill.

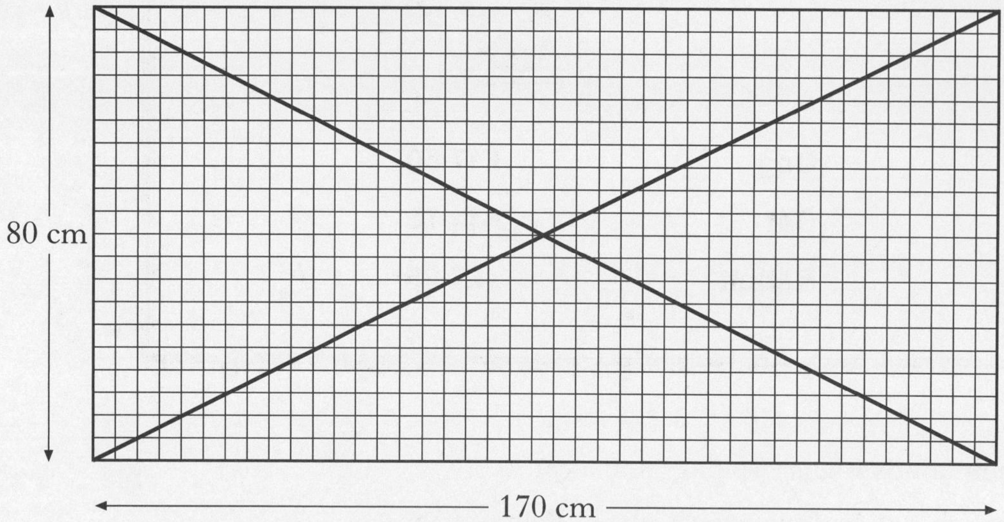

Find the length of one of the metal bars.

Round your answer to the nearest centimetre.

Do not use a scale drawing.

4

DO NOT WRITE IN THIS MARGIN

Marks KU RE

5. (*a*) Simplify

$$2(3x + 7) + 4(3 - x).$$

3

(*b*) Solve the inequality

$$4a - 3 \geq 21.$$

2

[Turn over

DO NOT WRITE IN THIS MARGIN

Marks | KU | RE

6. DEFG is a kite:

- angle DEG = 35 °
- EF = 14 centimetres.

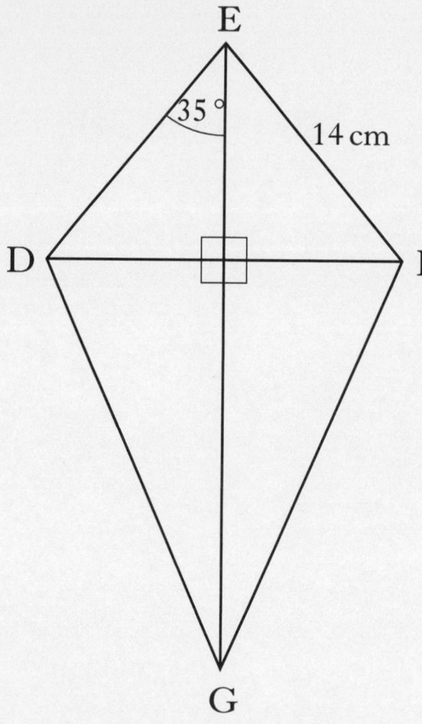

Calculate the length of DF.

4

DO NOT WRITE IN THIS MARGIN

Marks | KU | RE

7. A supermarket has a canopy over its entrance.

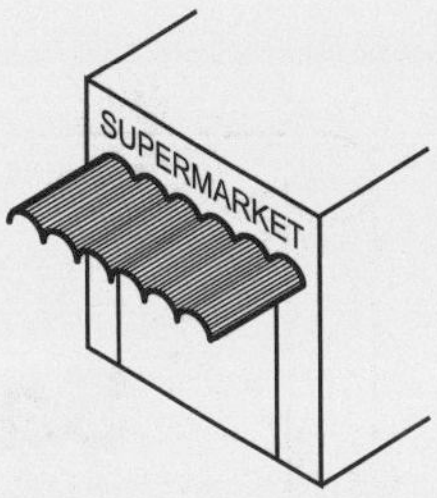

The edge of the canopy has 6 semicircles as shown below.

Each semicircle has a diameter of 4 metres.

(*a*) Find the length of the curved edge of **one of the semicircles**. 2

(*b*) Tony attaches fairy lights to the edge of the canopy.

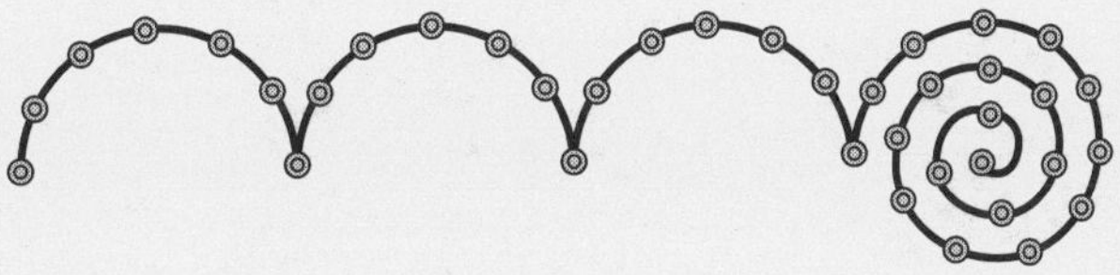

He has 40 metres of fairy lights.

Is this enough for the whole canopy?

Give a reason for your answer. 2

DO NOT WRITE IN THIS MARGIN

Marks | KU | RE

8.

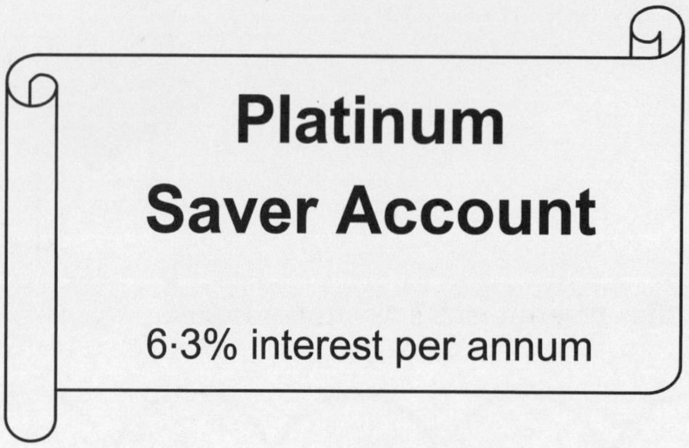

Sally invests £4200 in the Platinum Saver Account which pays 6·3% interest per annum.

How much simple interest will she receive after 10 months? **3**

DO NOT WRITE IN THIS MARGIN

Marks | KU | RE

9. In the diagram:

- O is the centre of the circle
- AC is a diameter
- B is a point on the circumference
- angle BAC = 43 °.

Calculate the size of shaded angle BOC.

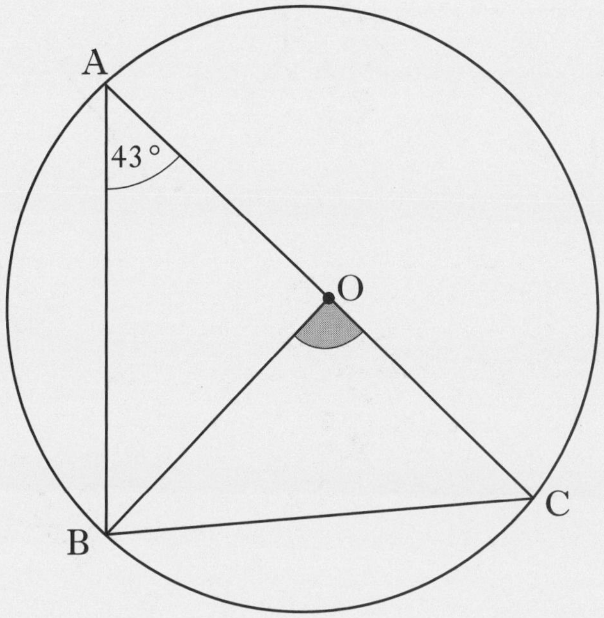

3

DO NOT WRITE IN THIS MARGIN

Marks | KU | RE

10. The end face of a grain hopper is shown in the diagram.

(*a*) Calculate the area of the end face.

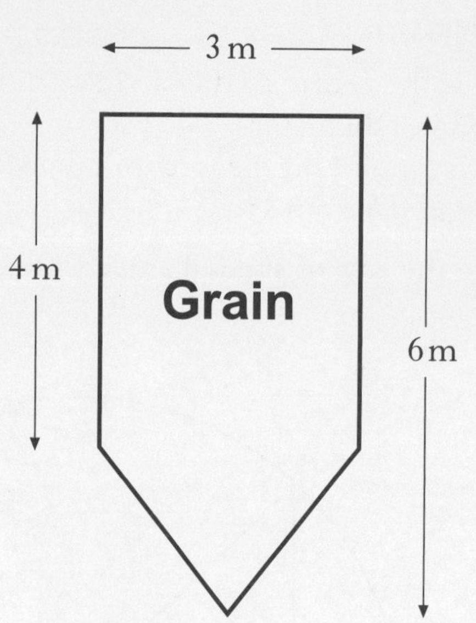

3

(*b*) The grain hopper is in the shape of a prism with a length of 3·5 metres.

Find the volume of the hopper.

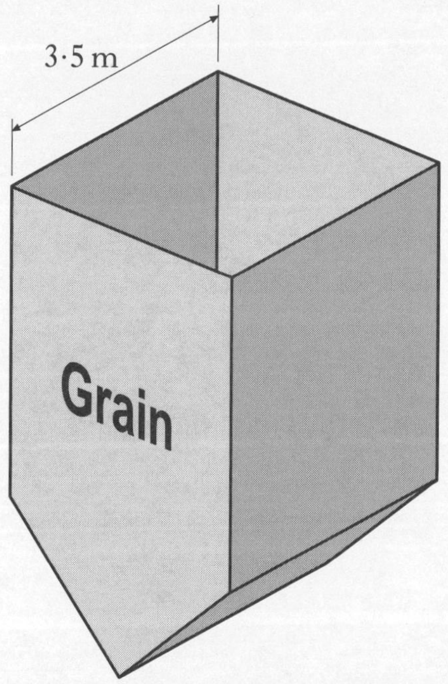

2

DO NOT WRITE IN THIS MARGIN

Marks | KU | RE

11. The diagram below shows the design for a house window.

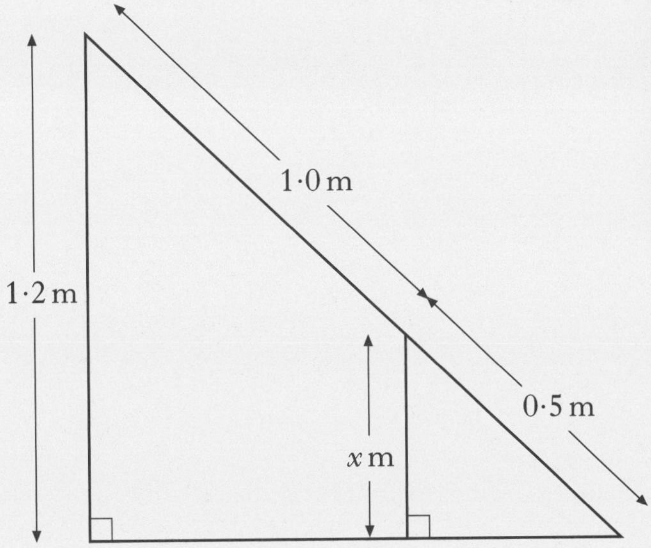

Find the value of x.

3

[Turn over for Question 12 on *Page fourteen*

DO NOT WRITE IN THIS MARGIN

Marks	KU	RE

12. The burning time, t minutes, of a candle varies directly as its height, h millimetres.

A candle with a height of 75 millimetres burns for 180 minutes.

(*a*) What is the burning time of a 40 millimetre candle? **3**

(*b*) A candle burns for $2\frac{1}{2}$ hours.

What is the height of this candle? **3**

[*END OF QUESTION PAPER*]

ADDITIONAL SPACE FOR ANSWERS

ADDITIONAL SPACE FOR ANSWERS

[BLANK PAGE]

[BLANK PAGE]

Pocket answer section for SQA General Mathematics 2003–2007

Published by Leckie & Leckie Ltd, 3rd Floor, 4 Queen Street, Edinburgh EH2 1JE
tel: 0131 220 6831, fax: 0131 225 9987, enquiries@leckieandleckie.co.uk, www.leckieandleckie.co.uk

Mathematics General Level—Paper 1 (Non-calculator) 2003

1. (*a*) 0·846

(*b*) 382·2

(*c*) 3·45

(*d*) $\frac{13}{16}$

2. 249°

3. $\frac{2}{9}$

4.

5. (*a*) 7·1

(*b*) 5·2

6. No (15% of £33 = £4·95. So the total should have been £37·95 which is less than £38·95.)

7. (*a*) –2 points

(*b*) 7 correct

8. 26 × 37

9. $7{\cdot}364 \times 10^9$

10. Angle BOE = 40°

Mathematics General Level—Paper 2 2003

1. 94·8 km/h

2. 15 hours

3. 4·2

4. Chicken + Puddings = 15·98
Chicken + Soups = 16·98
Fish + Puddings = 16·98
Fish + Soups = 17·98
Pasta + Soups + Puddings = 19·97

5. (*a*)

x	–4	0	4
y	**–9**	**–1**	**7**

(*b*)

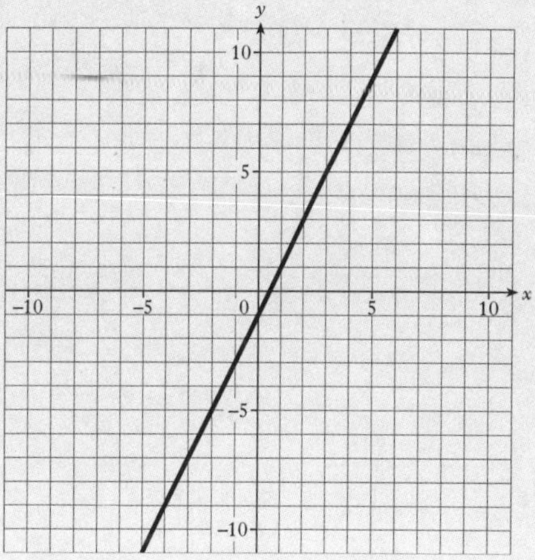

6. 24→43→36

7. 6·75 m

8. 18 candles

9. (*a*) 4*w* + 19

(*b*) *x* < 5

10. (*a*) £544

(*b*) 3·5 m

Mathematics General Level—Paper 2 2003 (cont.)

11. 8·01 m

12. 609 m

13. 240 m^2

Mathematics General Level—Paper 1 (Non-calculator) 2004

1. (*a*) 13·38

(*b*) 299·6

(*c*) 0·57

(*d*) £162

2. 0·43

3.

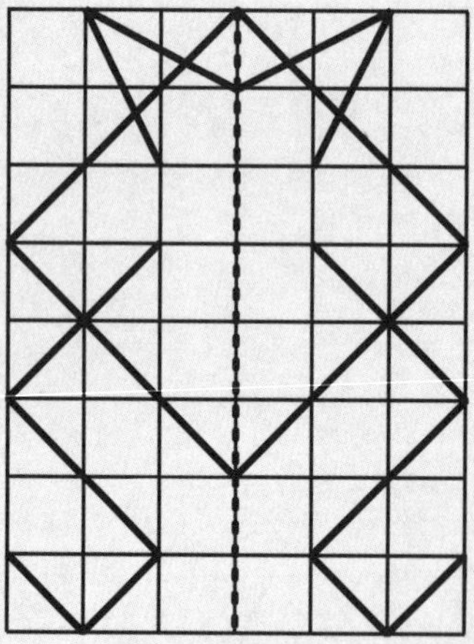

4. 181 300 000

5.

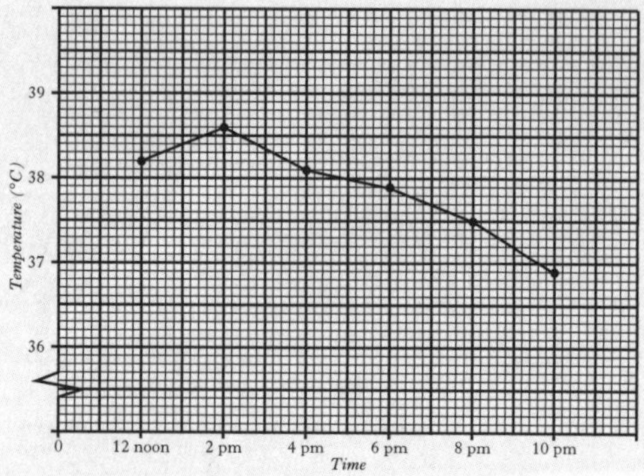

6. $^1/_4$

7. ∠DGF = 78°

8. 3498
3948
4938
9348
9438

9. 80 g sugar, 160 g butter

10. 8 (°C)

11. 2h 30 min

Mathematics General Level—Paper 2 2004

1. 198°

2. (*a*) 59·87

   (*b*) Yes with reason

3. 706·5 cm^3

4. (*a*) $x = 7$

   (*b*) $4(3 + 2p)$

5. Radius = 6·6 cm

6. 53·1°

7. (*a*) 755 Euros

   (*b*) 154·30 Sw.Fr.

8. 5·2 m^2

9. Sports channels

10. (*a*) £805

    (*b*) £69·30

    (*c*) £699·44

11. (*a*) £167·37

    (*b*) £75·11

    (*c*) 11 months

12. A 5 amp fuse is required

13.

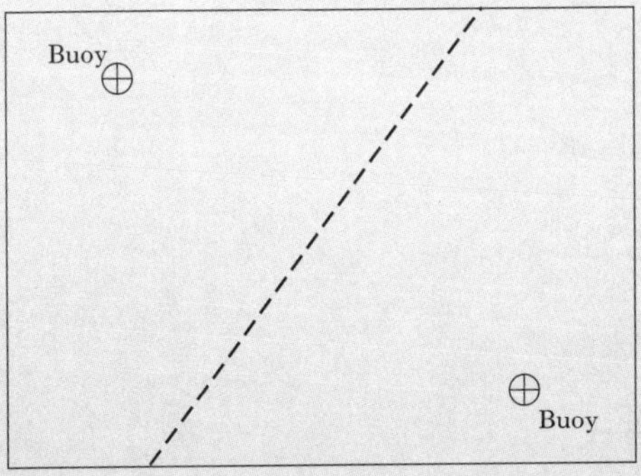

Mathematics General Level Paper 1 (Non-calculator) 2005

1. (*a*) 33·82

   (*b*) 5103

   (*c*) 46·3

   (*d*) 42 cm

2. 62°C

3. (*a*)

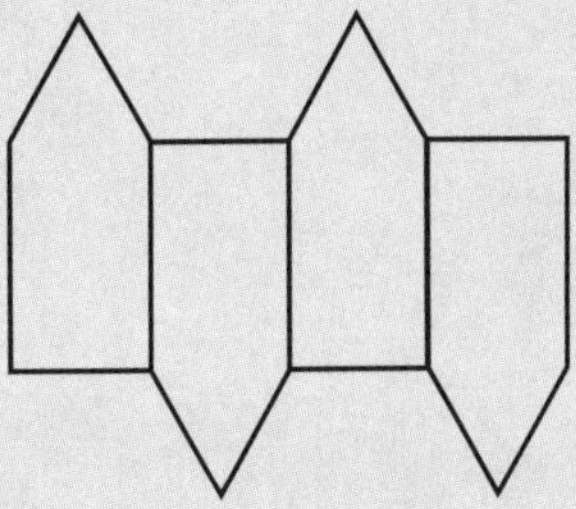

   (*b*)

Shape number(s)	1	2	3	4	5	6		13
Number of matches(m)	5	9	13	17	21	25		53

   (*c*) $m = 4s + 1$

   (*d*) 15

4. (*a*) £ 56 000 000

   (*b*) £ $5{\cdot}6 \times 10^7$

5.

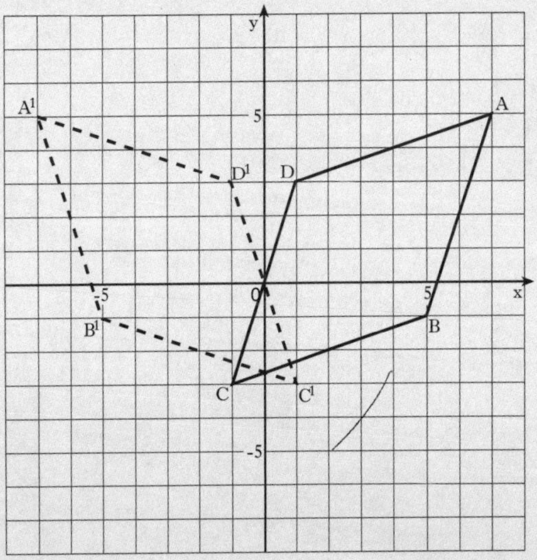

Mathematics General Level Paper 1 (Non-calculator) 2005 (cont.)

6. 2·04 kg/sq. cm

7. (*a*) 39 p

(*b*) £ 4·53

8. 25%

9. 105°

Mathematics General Level—Paper 2 2005

1. (*a*) 7 hours 30 minutes

(*b*) 85·9 km/h

2. (*a*)

1	1 7
2	0 5 5 5 5 6 6 8 9
3	1 2 2 2 3 5
4	1 2 3

(n=20 4 | 1=41)

(*b*) 25

3. (*a*) £ 556

(*b*) Big Computer Shop

4. 8·6 m

5. (*a*) $6x - 10$

(*b*) $x \geq 6$

6. £ 150 000

7. (*a*) 403

(*b*)

Cost of units:	£ 30·50
Sub Total:	39·71
VAT:	1·99
Total:	41·70

8. £ 5 000 000

9. Once
1st fill 780 km, 2nd fill 500 km

10. (*a*) 3·375 cm^3

(*b*) 48

11. 21·3°

12. 85·12 cm

Mathematics General Level—Paper 1 (Non-calculator) 2006

1. (*a*) 1·93

(*b*) 91 000

(*c*) 0·113

(*d*) 27·6 litres

2. £5·66

3. $\$3{\cdot}2 \times 10^8$

4. (*a*)

1	2	3	4	5
5	8		14	17

(*b*) $d = 3s + 2$

(*c*) (i) 30
(ii) 92

5. $-\frac{3}{8}$

6. (*a*) $\frac{3}{10}$

(*b*) $\frac{2}{7}$

7. (*a*) $3\frac{1}{2}$ hours

(*b*) $9\frac{1}{2}$ hours

8. (*a*)

1	0 5
2	3 5 5 8
3	0 2 3 4 5 8
4	1 2 4 6
5	2 5
6	2

(n = 19 1|5 = 15)

(*b*) 34

9. 14°

Mathematics General Level—Paper 2 2006

1. £1185

2. 270 pages

3.

6	0	0	0	30
5	1	0	0	28
5	0	1	0	27
5	0	0	1	25
4	1	1	0	25

4. 176·1 cm

5. 12 hours

6. (*a*) $3(2a + 5b)$

(*b*) $x = 8$

7. 10 min

8. 20·7 m

9. (*a*) 0·442

(*b*) twice

10. (*a*) £114

(*b*) No, it will cost her £6 more

Mathematics General Level—Paper 2 2006 (cont.)

11.

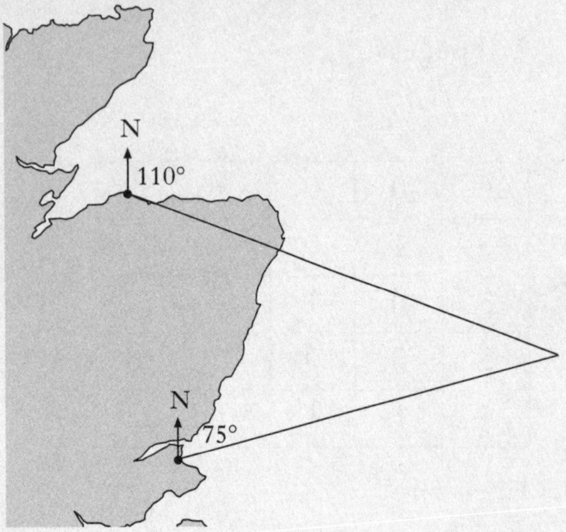

12. £55·08

Mathematics General Paper 1 2007 (non-calculator)

1. (*a*) 2·438

(*b*) 261·2

(*c*) 46·5

(*d*) $21\frac{2}{3}$

2. 0·000 23 s

3.

Weights	*Dance*	*Running*	*Cycling*	*Swimming*	*Total Time*
		✓	✓	✓	95
	✓	✓		✓	105
	✓	✓	✓		90
✓	✓			✓	100
✓			✓	✓	90
	✓		✓	✓	115

4.

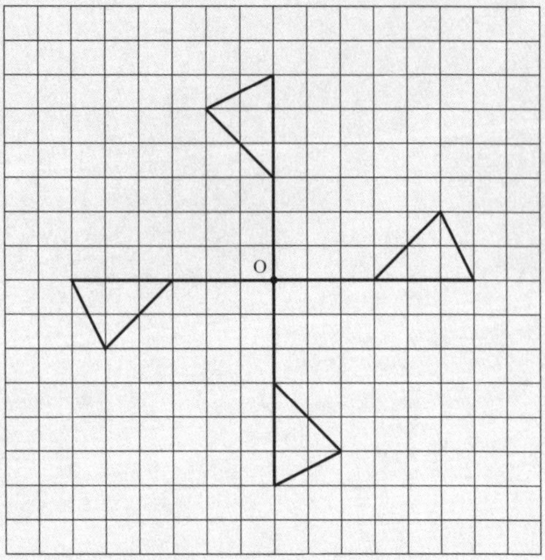

5. 34°

6. (*a*)

s	1	2	3	4	5		12
w	6	11	16	21	26		61

(*b*) $w = 5s + 1$

(*c*) $s = 16$

7. (*a*),(*b*)

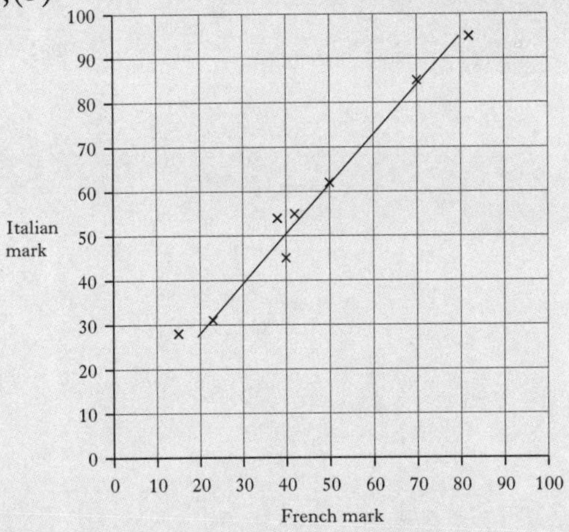

(*c*) Answer read from line (±2)

8. £61·75

9. (*a*) $\frac{3}{25}$

(*b*) $\frac{7}{24}$

10. 320

Mathematics General Paper 2 2007

1. 180 km

2. £4725

3. 3 times per year

4. 188 cm

5. (*a*) 2x + 26

(*b*) $a \geq 6$

6. 16·06 cm

7. (*a*) 6·28 m

(*b*) Yes, because 40 m (length available) is more than 37·7 m (length needed)

8. £220·50

9. 86°

10. (*a*) 15 m^2

(*b*) 52·5 m^3

11. 0·4

12. (*a*) 96 min

(*b*) 62·5 mm

25 29 33 37 41 45 49 53

25 28 33 ✓

29 33 37 41 45 49 53

m = 4S+1

=

61 = 4S + 1

61 − 1 = 4S

$\frac{61-1}{4}$ = S

$\frac{60}{4}$ = S

15 = S

20,000
2800
£ 56,000,000

Official SQA answers to ISBN 978-1-84372-518-3
2003–2007